SAY IT LIKE A KOREAN!

Korean HANGUL for Beginners

Learn to read, write and pronounce Korean plus hundreds of useful words and phrases!

Emily Curtis, Haewon Cho and Soohee Kim

TUTTLE Publishing

Tokyo | Rutland, Vermont | Singapore

Contents

Welcome to Hangul!

This is going to be a fun and enlightening path to reading and writing Korean. First step, imagine yourself fluently reading and writing a new kind of script!

한 국 말

The Korean writing system is called **Hangul** (also spelled **Hangeul**). You can easily learn to read and write Hangul, considered by some to be the most scientific writing system in the world. That is not just Korean pride; there is some objective truth to the claim, as Hangul was created thoughtfully and carefully by scholars just for the Korean language (unlike most other writing systems which developed slowly over time and then were borrowed for use with other languages).

While at first glance, Hangul might look like indecipherable circles and squares, it is very systematic and organized, and we will walk you through the few twists and turns that do inevitably exist when we try to write down a dynamic and changing language.

The most scientific script

You might hear people say that Korean is the most scientific language or refer to Hangul as the Korean *language*. This is a common confusion between a language and its writing system, while in fact, they are logically different entities. Not all languages in the world are written, even today. And, on the other hand, many different languages share the same writing system. For example, the Roman alphabet is used to write many languages around the world, especially European and African languages. Also, Koreans *spoke* the Korean language long before they wrote it; that is, long before Hangul was invented.

The Korean *language* is more accurately called **Hangungmal** or **Hangugeo.** This refers to the spoken language, its grammar and vocabulary, literature and news either written or spoken, etc. Can you speak Hangungmal?

The word Hangul refers to the writing itself, the letters and their arrangement on the page. (A related word is **gulsshi**, which just means "writing" (in the sense of something that is written, for example, "you have good handwriting" or "I can't read that writing"). Note that you can see the first part of the word, **gul**. Another related word, **guljja** means "a written character."

While Hangungmal the *language,* is no more scientific or organized than any other (spoken) language, Hangul, *the writing system*, is very scientific and easy to learn, as you will see.

Origins of Hangul

The writing system known as Hangul (한글) was invented in 1443 by King Sejong the Great (세종대왕), the fourth king of the Joseon Dynasty. Korean scholars had already been using Chinese characters for more than 1,500 years to write the Korean language, or at times, to write laws and records in Chinese. Books and personal letters were rare during that period, and common folks could not write at all. As he was a wise and compassionate king, Sejong wanted to create a writing system that everyone, not just scholars, could learn and put into practical use every day. Historians say that he and his scholars studied the human vocal tract anatomy and the way in which the sounds of language are produced. Then they made the letters reflect the phonetics of the sounds.

Another wonderful thing about Hangul is that it is an alphabet; in other words, it is a system in which each letter represents a single consonant sound or vowel sound. This is unlike the Chinese system, where each character represents a *word*. It is similar to English and the ABCs but it is much more consistent. Each vowel letter of Hangul represents a single, consistent sound—it doesn't matter what other sounds are nearby, ㅏ always represents **ah** as in *father*. (Compare English letter *a* in *father*, *cake* and *apple*, which has three completely sounds.) You don't have to memorize many irregular spellings when you are learning the Korean writing system.

Also, since Hangul is an alphabet, there are only 40 consonant and vowel letters to learn. (Originally there were 44 letters, of which 4 are not currently used.) Hangul is truly a *very* clever invention and a handy-dandy system to read and write!

King Sejong had a manual created, the Hunminjeongeum (훈민정음), to explain how the new alphabet worked. This manual has been designated as Korea's National Treasure item number 70, and was registered in 1997 as a UNESCO Memory of the World document.

It is interesting to note that although writing was done with brushes at the time when Hangul was invented, the writing system is very geometric by design, and includes circles, squares and right angles. Originally, Hangul was written using lines and dots, but in modern-day writing those dots have now changed into short lines or tick marks. In this book we will give you the chance to explore some different fonts and handwriting styles to truly appreciate its aesthetics.

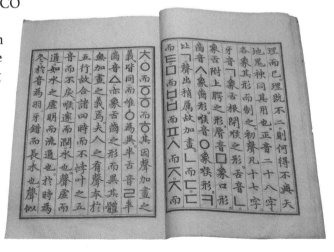

The basics of Hangul

The Hunminjeongeum claims that Hangul is easy to use, and it is! As mentioned, it is an alphabet, so there are few "characters" to learn—just 8 basic vowels and 10 basic consonants. If you count letters made by combining the basic ones, this comes to a total of 21 vowels and 19 consonants.

Basic Vowels

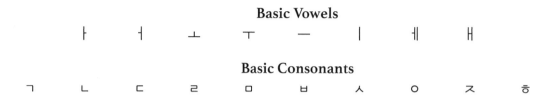

Basic Consonants

ㄱ   ㄴ   ㄷ   ㄹ   ㅁ   ㅂ   ㅅ   ㅇ   ㅈ   ㅎ

The consonant letters are shaped to represent the shape of the mouth while producing the given sound. For example, the letter ㅁ, which represents the sound **m**, is said to represent the shape of the closed lips used to produce the sound.

mmmwah!

The vowel letters were created to represent humankind, earth and sky in ways reminiscent of the Confucian philosophy of the time and to represent the vowels' grouping into yin and yang types. We won't talk more about this original symbolism but will instead provide mnemonic illustrations throughout the book that will help you remember the shapes of the letters.

The main twist that makes Hangul different from English writing is that instead of stringing all the letters along in a line (ㅎㅏㄴㄱㅜㄱㅁㅏㄹ), you need to arrange Hangul letters into blocks that represent the syllables:

It may look complicated at first, but rest assured there are only a few basic conventions to learn.

In the olden days, Hangul was read top-to-bottom, right–to-left, but the modern-day convention is to read it left-to-right, top-to-bottom. The letter strokes and the positioning of the letters in the syllable blocks are basically left-to-right, top-to-bottom as well.

There have been times when Hangul was mixed with **Hanja** (Chinese characters) to write the Korean language. Many, many words were borrowed from Chinese into Korean (still called **Han-ja-eo** ("Chinese character words")), and these were often written using Chinese characters. This practice was abandoned in the 1970s (in South Korea), and now these Sino-Korean words are written in Hangul.

It is not uncommon nowadays to see English and other European language words and names, especially on storefront signs, written in the Roman alphabet, mixed in among Hangul, but you will also find many such words written in Hangul as well. Many words of foreign origin have in fact been borrowed into the language.

Romanization

Romanization refers to using the Roman alphabet to write a language that is not normally written in that alphabet, like Korean. There have been a number of romanization systems utilized for writing Korean over the years. Korean governments often choose, mandate and update the system to use, and scholars may choose or create others.

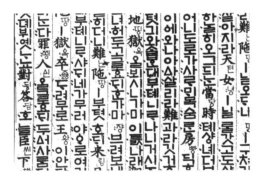

It is not our goal to give a detailed explanation of any of the romanization systems used for Korean, but the best known are the Revised Standard Romanization (the current South Korean government's system), McCune–Reischauer and Yale systems.

	한글	한국어	한국말
Revised	Hangeul	Hangugeo	Hangungmal
McCune–Reischauer	Han'gŭl	Han'gugŏ	Han'gungmal
Yale	Hankul	Hankwuke	Hankwungmal

No single romanization system is perfectly straightforward as a pronunciation guide nor as a one-to-one representation of Hangul spelling. In this book we use our own transliteration when talking about the sounds represented by Hangul letters. When introducing each letter we also give its Revised Standard Romanization. At the start of the book, we provide Revised Standard Romanization for unfamiliar words; but as you progress through the book and master the Hangul alphabet, our use of romanization decreases.

As romanization does not accurately capture actual pronunciation, we recommend you refer to the online audio files that accompany each exercise (see below) for accurate pronunciation of letters, syllables and words. The charts below are a basic guideline to how each Hangul letter is transcribed using the Revised Standard Romanization system. You can find out more about this system at korean.go.kr/front_eng/roman/roman_01.do

ㅏ	ㅓ	ㅗ	ㅜ	ㅡ	ㅣ	ㅐ	ㅔ
a	eo	o	u	eu	i	ae	e

ㅑ	ㅕ	ㅛ	ㅠ	ㅒ	ㅖ
ya	yeo	yo	yu	yae	ye

ㅚ	ㅟ	ㅘ	ㅙ	ㅝ	ㅞ	ㅢ
oe	wi	wa	wae	wo	we	ui

ㄱ	ㄴ	ㄷ	ㄹ	ㅁ	ㅂ	ㅅ	ㅇ	ㅈ
g, k *	n	d, t*	l, r **	m	b, p*	s	--/ng	j

ㅊ	ㅋ	ㅌ	ㅍ	ㅎ
ch	k	t	p	h

ㅃ	ㅉ	ㄸ	ㄲ	ㅆ
pp	jj	tt	kk	ss

* ㄱ, ㄷ and ㅂ are transcribed as **g, d** and **b** before a vowel; they are transcribed as **k, t** and **p** when they come before another consonant or as the last sound in a word.

** ㄹ is transcribed as **r** before a vowel and as **l** before a consonant or at the end of a word: a double ㄹ sound is transcribed as **ll**.

To access the online audio recordings and printable flash cards for this book

1. Check that you have an Internet connection.
2. Type the following URL into your web browser:
   tuttlepublishing.com/korean-hangeul-for-beginners

For support, you can email us at info@tuttlepublishing.com

SECTION ONE

LETTERS AND SYLLABLES

1 READING AND WRITING VOWELS

1.1 Vowel sounds and letters

The English vowel *letters* are *a, e, i, o* and *u*, but they represent a number of different *sounds*. The letter *a* represents three different vowel *sounds* in c*a*ke, f*a*ther and h*a*t, for example, even though we refer to the letter as *ay*. Korean vowel letters correspond to *one* sound each, regardless of other letters or sounds around them in the word, making reading and spelling Hangul a lot easier! *And the name of a vowel letter in Korean is just the sound that it represents, like **ah** or **oh**.*

What exactly is a vowel sound? When you make a vowel sound, as in the words *eye* or *oh*, your mouth is rather open and the air comes out easily, without anything blocking its free flow through the mouth. When you make a consonant sound, as at the beginning of the words *say* or *key*, the air is noticeably blocked somewhere in the mouth. Another way to think about it is that you can't sing a song clearly using only consonants, but we can follow a tune quite well if it is sung using vowels. This is the fundamental difference between vowel and consonant *sounds*.

Hangul *letters* represent this fundamental difference between consonants and vowels. King Sejong the Great made the consonant letters thinking about where in the mouth the main blocking of air happens. And he made vowel letters to represent a philosophical idea of the sounds themselves. The result of these different approaches to consonant and vowel sounds is that Hangul letters representing consonant sounds have more complex and angular shapes, while the vowel letters are usually two lines intersecting at a right angle.

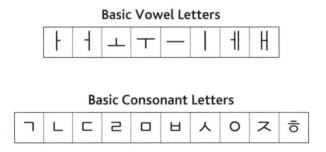

In this chapter, we focus on the letters representing basic vowel sounds.

1.2 Syllable boxes

As mentioned in the introduction, Korean letters are arranged into squares that represent syllables. A syllable is a beat in a word: for example, the word Hangul has two syllables: *Han* and *gul*. Korean words are spelled in syllable blocks or boxes.

In Korean, syllables may have only one vowel sound (V), or a consonant followed by a vowel (CV), or CV + a final consonant (CVC).

When a syllable starts with a vowel, without a consonant sound before it, a placeholder consonant is written before the vowel in the square: the letter ㅇ. When ㅇ comes before a vowel in a syllable, it is silent. So the way to write the syllable **ah**, with the vowel ㅏ, is ㅇ + ㅏ, that is, 아.

Some vowel-only syllables are written with the ㅇ on the left-hand side and some have the ㅇ on the top, above the vowel letter. We'll explain which vowels work which way as we go through the vowel letters now. Let's get used to writing Hangul syllables right from the start, as we learn the basic vowel sounds and letters.

1.3 Basic vowels

In the top left of each section, romanization of each letter is given using the Korean government's Revised Standard Romanization (see page 8). In the explanatory text, we use our own transliteration, to help you achieve correct pronunciation. Use the online audio files (see page 8) too!

The letter ㅏ represents a vowel sound similar to the **ah** in *father*, *hot* and *odd* in North American English pronunciation, or the **ah** sound you make when you are relaxing or when the doctor is checking your throat.

To remember this letter, imagine a face turned to the right, and ㅏ as a signpost pointing out of the mouth. ㅏ is written with a long vertical stroke then a short horizontal stroke on the right, starting from the center of the first vertical stroke. The lines should touch but not cross, and they should form a right angle.

aah!

 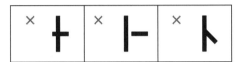

We will practice this ㅏ vowel in a syllable. Remember that ㅇ is silent, so the sound of the syllable is still **ah.** This applies to all the vowel syllables we will practice in this section.

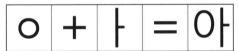

Trace this syllable in different font styles and then practice on your own.

🎧 **Listen to the audio recording, repeat the syllable above and the words below, then practice tracing and writing the missing syllables.**

아가 **aga** baby

아빠 **appa** dad

eo

The letter ㅓ represents a vowel sound between the **au** in *caught* and the **uh** in *cut* or *huh*. The jaw drops much lower for ㅏ [**ah**] than for this sound, but both are made far back in the mouth, or, it may feel like this one comes from the throat.

This letter is easily confused with ㅏ. One way to remember ㅓ is to think of the image of the vowel starting from deep in the back of your mouth and there is a stick pointing into your mouth toward that throaty place.

aaw/uh

The letter ㅓ is written by making a short horizontal stroke toward the right, starting from the center of the letter-writing space and then making a long vertical stroke that meets it. Be sure to make the lines perpendicular and not let them cross each other.

   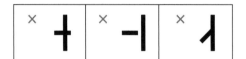

We will practice this ㅓ vowel in a syllable.

ㅇ + ㅓ = 어

Trace this syllable in different font styles and then practice on your own.

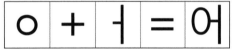

🎧 **Listen to the audio recording, repeat the syllable above and the words below, then practice tracing and writing the missing syllables.**

어머니 **eomeoni** mother

영어 **yeongeo** English

ㅗ

The letter ㅗ makes a sound similar to the vowel in *boat*, *goal* and *no* but it should not end in a **w**-like mouth position or be made into two syllables, like when you insist "no-wuh!" It should be a pure **o** sound, as in the Spanish *no*.

One way to remember this letter is to think of a thumb pointing upwards: "*Oh!* Impressive!"

Oh! ☺

The letter ㅗ is written by making a short vertical stroke top to bottom, then making a long horizontal stroke that meets it at its center. Be sure that the lines of the stroke meet up, are perpendicular and do not cross.

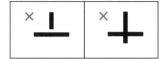

We will practice this ㅗ vowel in a syllable.

$$\text{O} \quad + \quad \text{ㅗ} \quad = \quad \text{오}$$

Trace this syllable in different font styles and then practice on your own.

🎧 **Listen to the audio recording, repeat the syllable above and the words below, then practice tracing and writing the missing syllables.**

오 five

오이 **oi** cucumber

오이

ㅜ
u

The letter ㅜ represents a sound similar to the one in the English words *too*, *who* and *loop* and should be made with the lips sticking out and very rounded. You cannot make this Korean sound while smiling!

This letter is easily confused with ㅗ (**o**). One way to remember ㅜ is to think of it as a thumb pointing downwards: "Booooo! No good!"

To make the letter ㅗ, make the horizontal line first, then add a vertical tick downwards from the center of the first line.

boooo!

We will practice this ㅜ vowel in a syllable.

$$O + ㅜ = 우$$

Trace this syllable in different font styles and then practice on your own.

Listen to the audio recording, repeat the syllable above and the words below, then practice tracing and writing the missing syllables.

우주 **uju** universe

우유 **uyu** milk

eu

The letter — represents a vowel sound similar to the one in *good* but said without sticking out your lips. Say it while smiling or pulling your lips to the sides. You may also think of it as a sound you'd make if disgusted or punched in the stomach, but to Koreans it is a very pretty sound. Since there is no corresponding English vowel sound or letter, we will use **eu** to represent this Korean letter.

One way to remember this letter is to imagine a stick pinched between your teeth as you say this sound, or the way your lips spread to the sides.

The letter — is written by making a long horizontal stroke left to right. That's it! Just don't make it too crooked, curved or short.

"eu"

We will practice this — vowel in a syllable.

Trace this syllable in different font styles and then practice on your own.

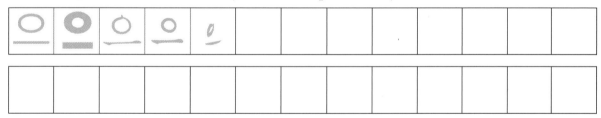

 This vowel usually occurs after a consonant, but here is one case of the simple vowel-sound syllable. Listen to the audio recording, repeat the syllable above and the word below, then practice tracing and writing the missing syllable.

으깨다 **ukkaeda** to mash

The letter ㅣ is like the vowel sound in the words *pizza*, *Tina* and <u>see</u>. This letter may be easy to remember because it looks like the *i* in *pizza* and *Tina*. Also, the word for *teeth* in Korean is **ee** and you need to show all your teeth when saying ㅣ .

The letter ㅣ is written by making a long vertical stroke, top to bottom. That's it! Try not to make it crooked, curved or too short. To remember the shape of this letter, imagine smiling with a tooth-pick near your front teeth.

'ee'

We will practice this ㅣ vowel in a syllable.

ㅇ + ㅣ = 이

Trace this syllable in different font styles and then practice on your own.

🎧 **Listen to the audio recording, repeat the syllable above and the words below, then practice tracing and writing the missing syllables.**

이 teeth

오이 cucumber

On the next two pages you will find two more vowel letters that are considered "basic," because they represent single vowel sounds.

ㅐ	
ae	Add the letter ㅣ to ㅏ and you get ㅐ, which represents a vowel sound somewhere between the vowel in *bet* and the vowel in *wait*. Some books might say that it is like the vowel in *bad*, but that is not true for today's Korean speakers.

One way to remember this letter is to think that it looks like an H ("aitch").

The letter ㅐ is made by writing an ㅏ (vertical stroke top to bottom, then horizontal tick left to right), then making a vertical stroke to the right, meeting the horizontal tick of the ㅏ. The right-hand vertical line is usually just a little longer than the left-hand line. Be sure that your vertical lines are parallel and that they meet the tick at a right angle without a gap or crossing lines.

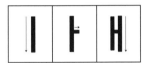 

... F G ㅐ I

letter "aitch"

We will practice this ㅐ vowel in a syllable.

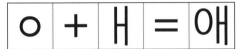

ㅇ + ㅐ = 애

Trace this syllable in different font styles and then practice on your own.

애	애	애	애	애						

🎧 **Listen to the audio recording, repeat the syllable above and the words below, then practice tracing and writing the missing syllables.**

애 child

애	

우애 brotherly love

|
e

Add the letter ㅣ to ㅓ and you get ㅔ which represents a vowel sound somewhere between the vowel in *head* and the vowel in *say* but without the smile at the end or the extra *yuh* sound. That is, it should not be possible to make it into two syllables (*say-ee* or *say-yuh*). It should be a pure vowel like in Spanish (*yo lo*) *se* ("I know it").

First make ㅓ, then make a parallel vertical stroke to the right. The right-hand line is usually a little longer than the left. Be sure the lines are parallel and the left one meets the tick at a right angle without a gap or crossing lines. We can't think of a good mnemonic for this, so how about "eh? I have no ideas!"

eh?

We will practice this ㅔ vowel in a syllable.

$$ ㅇ + ㅔ = 에 $$

Trace this syllable in different font styles and then practice on your own.

🎧 **Listen to the audio recording, repeat the syllable above and the words below, then practice reading and writing the missing syllables.**

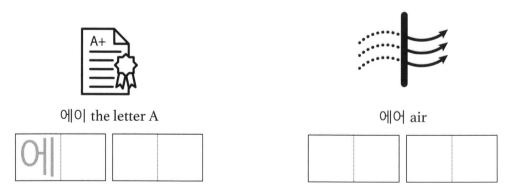

에이 the letter A   에어 air

For all practical purposes, ㅔ sounds the same as ㅐ in today's (Seoul) Korean. Some books say ㅐ is like the vowel in *bat* and ㅔ is like the vowel in *bet*. Others say ㅐ is like the vowel in *bet* and ㅔ is like the vowel in *bait*. An English speaker is best off pronouncing both ㅐ and ㅔ like the vowel in *bet*. When you hear a Korean word using one of these vowels, you may have to find out and then memorize whether the word is spelled ㅏ + ㅣ (ㅐ) or ㅓ + ㅣ (ㅔ).

1.4 All together!

Now you know how to write all the basic vowels in syllables with a placeholder consonant ○. Let's review and polish your skills.

As we have seen, when the vowel letter has a longer vertical line, like ㅏ, ㅓ, ㅣ, ㅐ and ㅔ, the ○ is written to the left of the vowel: 아, 어, 이, 애 and 에.

The ○ letter in this case is made a bit longer top-to-bottom than it is wide, but it does not take up all the space in the left side of the syllable box. Be sure not to make the circle letter overlap the vowel letter, and remember that we are dividing one syllable box in half. The letter ○ is written counter-clockwise. Here is an example with 아.

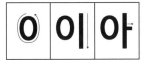 

When the vowel letter has a longer horizontal line, like ㅗ, ㅜ and ㅡ do, the ○ is written above the vowel letter: 오, 우 and 으.

In order to make the box more square, the ○ letter is often made shorter, top-to-bottom and wider to fill the space above a letter with a long horizontal line. The two letters also are adjusted to be centered in the top and bottom halves of the square.

Practice 1 ✍ **Trace these syllables in different font styles then practice on your own. Notice how the ○ takes up its own half of the syllable box.**

아	**아**	아	아	아						
어	**어**	어	어	어						
이	**이**	이	이	이						
애	**애**	애	애	애						
에	**에**	에	에	에						

✍ Trace these syllables in different font styles then practice on your own. Notice how the ㅇ is centered in its own (top) half of the syllable box.

오	**오**	오	오	오							
우	**우**	우	우	우							
으	**으**	으	으	으							

Practice 3 Cover the first column of the chart, look at the second and try to think where the ㅇ should be written with each vowel. Then cover up the second and third columns, and see if you can read the syllables in the first column.

Syllable	Vowel	Vowel sound
아	ㅏ	**ah** as in *father* (notice how the ㅏ letter points out from the mouth)
어	ㅓ	**au** as in *caught* or **uh** as in *cut* (notice how the ㅓ letter points into the mouth)
오	ㅗ	**o** as in *no* (with no *wuh* at the end)
우	ㅜ	**oo** as in *moo* said with both lips sticking really far out
으	─	like the vowel in *good*, said while smiling
이	ㅣ	**ee** as in *see* or *Tina*
애	ㅐ	**eh** as in *bed*
에	ㅔ	**eh** as in *bed* or **ai** as in *bait*

Practice 4 Practice reading these vowel syllables. The top row has the syllables in random order; the second row is organized in pairs that are easily confused when reading.

오	어	애	아	이	으	에	우
o	ah/uh	eh	ah	ee	eu (as in *good*)	eh	oo

아	어	오	우	으	이	에	애
ah/uh	au/uh	o	oo	eu (as in *good*)	ee	eh	eh

Korean does not have contrasting short and long vowels nor does it have particularly short-ened or extended vowels. When you pronounce 오, 우 or 에, for example, you should not slide into a **w** or **y** sound at the end as in the English words *no*, *ew* or *hey*. (Think about how it is possible to make the word no into two syllables when you are insisting: "no-wuh!") This is not possible in Korean. To make the Korean vowel sounds, try to make a pure vowel sound, as in the Spanish words *bueno* or *olé* (if you know how to), keeping the shape of your lips and tongue constant all the way through the vowel sound. No *wuh* at the end!

Nor should you say Korean vowels staccato or with an abrupt stop at the end. Try listening to how Koreans say 네 for "yes." Unlike the English *yep*, it isn't usually shortened so strikingly.

1.4.1 Vowel harmony

Vowels in Korean are grouped into yin vowels ("dark vowels") and yang vowels ("bright vowels").

The vowel syllables above with a white background behave similarly in Korean grammar and give a feeling of lightness, smallness, brightness or intensity in certain vocabulary words. The vowel syllables with a gray background work together in certain grammar patterns, and give a heavy, big, dark or diffused nuance. (Note that 이 is a neutral vowel.)

There used to be what is called "vowel harmony" in the Korean language whereby the vowels in a suffix had to match the vowels in the word it was attached to, so that the vowels in a word were either all yang or all yin vowels. Although strict vowel harmony has more or less died away, the phenomenon remains in modern standard Korean in certain words and verb conjugations. We also see the yin and yang nuance in onomatopoeic words:

반짝 [**panjjak**] with bright yang vowel ㅏ means *twinkle*, *glint*, *glitter*, *sparkle* of shining stars, for example

vs.

번쩍 [**puhnjjuhk**] with dark yin vowel ㅓ means *glare*, *flash*, *gleam* of thunder and headlights

깡총 [**ggangchong**] with ㅏ and ㅗ bright yang vowels means *hop*, describing a rabbit's hopping

vs.

껑충 [**gguhngchoong**] with ㅓ and ㅜ dark yin vowels means *jump*, *leap* describing a kangaroo's (bigger, heavier) jump

1.4.2 Practice

Practice 1 Practice tracing and writing these syllables.

아	○	+	ㅏ	=	아	아						
어	○	+	ㅓ	=	어	어						
오	○	+	ㅗ	=	오	오						
우	○	+	ㅜ	=	우	우						
으	○	+	ㅡ	=	으	으						
이	○	+	ㅣ	=	이	이						
애	○	+	ㅐ	=	애	애						
에	○	+	ㅔ	=	에	에						

Practice 2 Listen to the audio recording and circle the syllable or word you hear. See page 126 for answers.

1. 아   어   2. 이   으   3. 우   오   4. 어   우

5. 아이   오이   6. 우아   으아   7. 에   어   8. 에이   아이

Practice 3 Listen to the audio recording and fill in the blanks. See page 126 for answers.

the letter A

mother

milk

1. | | |
|---|---|

2. | 머 | 니 |
|---|---|

3. | | 유 |
|---|---|

2 COMPLEX VOWEL SYLLABLES

There are 13 more vowel syllables in Korean, known as complex vowel syllables. They are combinations of **y** as in *you* or **w** as in *we* plus another vowel afterwards. (So, yes indeed, **y** and **w** are spelled with vowel letters in Korean!)

2.1 Reading and writing complex vowel syllables

There are just a couple of basic tricks to writing **y**- and **w**-based complex vowel syllables, and the following section will help you master them easily.

2.1.1 y-based complex vowel syllables

ya

The super simple trick to writing complex vowel syllables that start with **y** is to add an extra short stroke parallel to the one that the basic letter has. For example, ㅏ has a short horizontal stroke to the right of the long vertical stroke. Make the tall vertical stroke first, then double that short horizontal tick to get ㅑ [**ya**], as in *yacht*. Try to make your ticks parallel and the same length, and be sure they meet up with the vertical stroke but do not cross it.

Be sure to follow the correct stroke order. We will practice this ㅑ vowel in a syllable.

Just like with ㅏ, the placeholder consonant ㅇ goes to the left of ㅑ. Trace this syllable in different font styles and then practice on your own.

🎧 **Listen to the audio recording, repeat the syllable above and the words below, then practice tracing and writing the missing syllables.**

아야 Ouch!

야구 **yagu** baseball

yeo

y + ㅓ works the same way: double up the short tick of ㅓ, that is, add a short tick parallel to the one already on ㅓ to get ㅕ [**yuh**] as in *yuck*.

Writing left to right, make the short ticks first: top, then bottom, then add the long vertical stroke to the right, meeting the ticks. Try to make your ticks parallel and the same length and be sure they meet up with the vertical stroke but do not cross it.

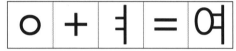

We will practice this ㅕ vowel in a syllable.

Just like with ㅓ, the placeholder consonant ㅇ goes to the left of ㅕ. Trace this syllable in different font styles and then practice on your own.

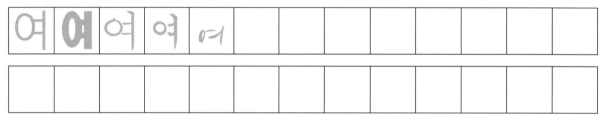

🎧 **Listen to the audio recording, repeat the syllable above and the words below, then practice tracing and writing the missing syllables.**

여우 fox

여자 **yeoja** woman

yo

How should we write **yo**? Since it is a **y**-based complex vowel syllable, it should have a doubled-up short stroke added to the basic vowel, ㅗ, with a short vertical tick to get ㅛ [yo] as in *yogurt*.

Writing top to bottom, make two parallel vertical ticks first, then add the bottom horizontal stroke. Be sure the ticks meet up with the horizontal stroke and do not cross it.

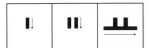

We will practice this ㅛ vowel in a syllable.

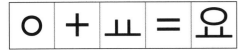

Just like with ㅗ, the placeholder consonant ㅇ goes above ㅛ. Trace this syllable in different font styles and then practice on your own.

🎧 **Listen to the audio recording, repeat the syllable above and the words below, then practice tracing and writing the missing syllables.**

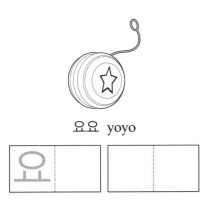

요요 yoyo

요가 **yoga** yoga

ㅠ

yu

How about **yu**? Just like the other **y**-based complex vowels, we add a short tick parallel to the one in the basic vowel. The basic vowel is ㅜ, with a short vertical tick at the bottom, so we write an ㅜ and add the extra tick to get ㅠ [**yu**], as in *you*.

Be sure the ticks meet up with the horizontal stroke and do not cross it.

We will practice this ㅠ vowel in a syllable.

ㅇ + ㅠ = 유

The Korean word for *milk* is 우유. Can you read that?

Just like with ㅜ, the placeholder consonant ㅇ goes above ㅠ. Trace this syllable in different font styles and then practice on your own.

유 유 유 유 유

🎧 **Listen to the audio recording, repeat the syllable above and the words below, then practice tracing and writing the missing syllables.**

이유 reason

유

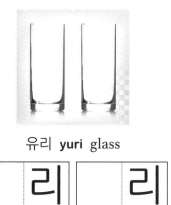

유리 **yuri** glass

리   리

yae ㅒ

Where is the short tick in the syllable ㅐ? It is between the two vertical strokes, right? To write its y-based counterpart, double up that short horizontal stroke in the middle, and you get ㅒ [**yeh**] as in *yellow*.

Try to make your ticks parallel and the same length and be sure they meet up with the horizontal strokes but do not cross.

We will practice this ㅐ vowel in a syllable.

Just like with ㅏ, the placeholder consonant ㅇ goes to the left of ㅐ. Trace this syllable in different font styles and then practice on your own.

🎧 **Listen to the audio recording, repeat the syllable above and the words below, then practice tracing and writing the missing syllables.**

애 this child

애기 **yaegi** talking

| 기 | | 기 |

ye

Lastly, how do you write the **y**-based complex vowel syllable based on ㅔ? Double-up that short horizontal stroke on the left, then make the two long vertical strokes: ㅖ [**yeh**], as in *yes*.

Be sure to follow the correct stroke order.

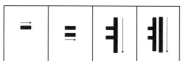

We will practice this ㅖ vowel in a syllable.

Just like with ㅔ, the placeholder consonant ㅇ goes to the left of ㅖ. Trace this syllable in different font styles and then practice on your own.

🎧 **Listen to the audio recording, repeat the syllable above and the words below, then practice tracing and writing the missing syllables.**

예 example

서예 **seoye** calligraphy

There are no **y**-based counterparts to ㅣ and ㅡ. These are combinations of sounds you will not hear in Korean.

2.1.2 Review

Cover the right-hand column showing **y**-based complex vowel syllables, as well as the chart at the bottom of this page. Look at the basic vowel syllable in the first column and try to write its **y**-based complex vowel syllable counterpart in the second column. Uncover the right-hand column and check your work.

Basic vowel syllable	y-based complex vowel syllable	
아		야
어		여
오		요
우		유
으		(no such vowel syllable in Korean)
이		(no such vowel syllable in Korean)
애		얘
에		예

2.1.3 Practice

Practice 1   Practice tracing and writing these complex vowel syllables.

야	○	+	ㅑ	=	야	야					
여	○	+	ㅕ	=	여	여					
요	○	+	ㅛ	=	요	요					
유	○	+	ㅠ	=	유	유					
얘	○	+	ㅒ	=	얘	얘					
예	○	+	ㅖ	=	예	예					

1. 야　　　여　　　　　2. 요　　　　유

3. 어　　　여　　　　　4. 우　　　　유

5. 예　　　에　　　　　6. 얘기　　　아기

Practice 3 Listen to the audio recording and fill in the blanks. See page 126 for answers.

milk

1. 우

fox

2. 우

yoga

3. 가

example

4.

talking

5. 기

baseball

6. 구

Practice 4

Find some Korean text online and try to spot any **y**-based complex vowel syllables. Compare different fonts. Are the ticks always parallel? Are they always the same length? Do they always touch the placeholder ㅇ or not touch it? Try imitating some of the font styles that you like best.

2.1.4 w-based complex vowel syllables

The **w** sound, as in *wink*, is written using vowel letters in Korean. Some of these **w**-based complex vowels use ⊥ to write the **w** part and some use ㅜ. The sounds **woo**, **woe** and **w** + — are not possible in Korean, so there is no way to write them in Hangul. At the end of this section we will also learn the complex vowel 의 , which is pronounced in two different ways depending on where it comes in the word.

wi

This vowel has the sound **wee** as in *weasel* or *week*. The **w** part is written using ㅜ. If you make the ㅜ sound followed quickly by ｜, it sounds like **wee**, so it makes sense to write it as ㅜ + ｜ .

Writing left to right, the ㅜ is written first, then the ｜ is written to the right. Make sure all strokes are vertical or horizontal, perpendicular and parallel. It is OK for the ㅜ to touch the ｜ , but be sure the strokes don't cross. We will practice this ㅟ vowel in a syllable.

The placeholder consonant ㅇ goes above the ㅜ. Trace this syllable in different font styles and then practice on your own.

🎧 Listen to the audio recording, repeat the syllable above and the words below, then practice tracing and writing the missing syllables.

위 above

가위 **gawi** scissors

ㅝ
WO

w + ㅓ is also written using ㅜ, with ㅓ to the right, "tucked in," and the ticks from ㅜ and ㅓ sharing some space. This vowel is pronounced **wuh** as in *wonder*.

Make sure all strokes are vertical or horizontal, perpendicular and parallel. Be sure the strokes don't cross. Notice that the horizontal stroke of ㅜ is a little shorter to make room for ㅓ on the right-hand side. We will practice this ㅝ vowel in a syllable.

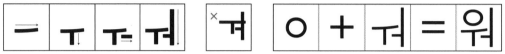

The placeholder consonant ㅇ goes above the ㅜ. Trace this syllable in different font styles and then practice on your own.

워 워 워 워 워

🎧 **Listen to the audio recording, repeat the syllable above and the words below, then practice tracing and writing the missing syllables.**

타워 **tawo** tower

타 워 타

샤워 **syawo** shower

샤 샤

Note 위 and 워 can be confused if you read too fast or the font is small. Try reading these—carefully, then faster and faster in random order:

워 위 위 워 위 위 워 위 위 워
위 위 워 워 워 위 워 위 위 워

wa

For **w** + ㅏ , **w** cannot be written with ㅜ because of Vowel Harmony (see page 21). ㅏ is a bright yang vowel, so cannot be paired with dark yin vowel ㅜ. This vowel, which makes the sound **wa**, as in *water*, uses ㅗ for the **w** sound, followed by ㅏ on the right.

A computer keyboard will not put ㅗ and ㅏ together in one complex vowel syllable: 오ㅏ.

The strokes can touch, but they should not cross. The horizontal stroke of ㅗ is a little shorter to make room for ㅏ to be on the right-hand side. We will practice this ㅘ vowel in a syllable.

 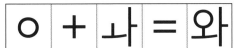

The placeholder consonant ㅇ goes above the ㅗ on the left side of the syllable box and the ㅏ goes on the right side. Trace this syllable in different font styles and then practice on your own.

와 **와** 와 와 와

 Listen to the audio recording, repeat the syllable above and the words below, then practice tracing and writing the missing syllables.

와이 the letter Y

와

하와이 **hawai** Hawaii

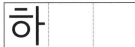
하   하

Another way to remember ㅗ + ㅏ and ㅜ + ㅓ is that there should never be two ticks pointing inward (to the middle of the syllable block), nor outward.
   오 + ㅓ would have two ticks pointing toward the ㅇ. Oh no!
   우 + ㅏ would have two ticks pointing away from the ㅇ. Oh no!
Stick to 와 and 워. (This was not necessarily the intention of the creators of Hangul, but it works as a mnemonic trick!)

ᅰ
we

Since ㅔ is based on ㅓ, in order to make its **w**-based mate, we use ㅜ to make ㅞ [**weh**], as in the word *weather*.

Write ㅜ first on the left, then add ㅔ, tucking in the ticks together. The top stroke of ㅜ can touch ㅔ, but the tick of ㅔ should not touch the tick of ㅜ.

We will practice this ㅞ vowel in a syllable.

The placeholder consonant ㅇ goes above the ㅜ. Notice that the horizontal stroke of ㅜ is a little shorter to make room for ㅔ to be on the right-hand side, even though the tick of ㅔ is tucked in under the bar of ㅜ. Trace this syllable in different font styles and then practice on your own.

웨	**웨**	웨	웨	웨								

🎧 **Listen to the audio recording, repeat the syllable above and the words below, then practice tracing and writing the missing syllables.**

웨이브 **weibeu** wave

웨이터 **weiteo** waiter

wae

Since ㅐ is based on ㅏ, we use the matching bright yang vowel ㅗ to make its w-based mate. Just like ㅗ + ㅏ = ㅘ [**wah**], ㅗ + ㅐ = ㅙ [**weh**], as in *weather*.

Be sure to follow the correct stroke order.

We will practice this ㅙ vowel in a syllable.

The placeholder consonant ㅇ goes above the ㅗ on the left side of the syllable box and the ㅐ goes on the right side. Trace this syllable in different font styles and then practice on your own.

왜	**왜**	왜	왜	왜							

🎧 **Listen to the audio recording, repeat the syllable above and the words below, then practice reading and writing the missing syllable.**

왜 why

왜	

oe

It is possible to add ㅗ + ㅣ into a complex vowel syllable (because ㅣ is a neutral vowel, neither yin nor yang), but when we do, the pronunciation is a bit unexpected. It is pronounced **weh**, as in *weather*, the same as the two preceding vowels.

To write this complex vowel, make the ㅗ on the left, slightly more narrow than usual, and then write ㅣ on the right. It is OK for the base stroke of ㅗ to touch ㅣ but it shouldn't cross it.

If you know the Korean surname Choi, this can help you remember this weird spelling. The name is spelled C-h-o-i because it is written with ㅚ in Hangul. But it is pronounced **chweh** in Korean.

Be sure to follow the correct stroke order. We will practice this ㅚ vowel in a syllable.

The placeholder consonant ㅇ goes above the ㅗ on the left side of the syllable box and the ㅣ goes on the right side. Trace this syllable in different font styles and then practice on your own.

외	**외**	외	외	외					

🎧 **Listen to the audio recording, repeat the syllable above and the words below, then practice reading and writing the missing syllable.**

야외 outdoors

외워요 memorize

2.1.4.1　Review: the three ways

Can you remember the three different ways that the sound **weh** might be spelled in Hangul? Did you come up with ㅗ + ㅐ = ㅙ, ㅜ + ㅔ = ㅞ and the crazy one, ㅗ + ㅣ = ㅚ?

Which way a word is spelled is a matter of memorizing. The word *why* is spelled 왜 [weh]. The last name Choi is spelled 최 [chweh] (with ㅚ in it). The phrase 웬일 [wehn-nil], "Why in the world?" or "What's up with this?" is spelled with ㅞ. The spellings are not interchangeable.

☞ **Practice reading the w-based syllables. Pay attention to the pronunciation in the brackets.**

워	위	웨	왜	외
[wuh]/[wau]	[wee]	[weh]	[weh]	[weh]
위	워	와	외	왜
[wee]	[wuh]/[wau]	[wah]	[weh]	[weh]
웨	위	워	웨	워
[weh]	[wee]	[wuh]/[wau]	[weh]	[wuh]/[wau]

ㅢ	The last complex vowel syllable is — + ㅣ. Remember that — is a sound like the vowel in *good* said while smiling (pulling the lips to the sides). It is neither a **y**-based nor a **w**-based complex vowel syllable: it is its own unique combination of — + ㅣ. But it is very rarely pronounced with the — sound in it. It is usually just pronounced ㅣ [**ee**] and occasionally ㅔ [**eh**].
ui	

To write it, make the — on the left, slightly more narrow than usual, and then write ㅣ on the right. It is OK for the horizontal stroke — to touch the vertical stroke ㅣ but it shouldn't cross it. We will practice this ㅢ vowel in a syllable.

The placeholder consonant ㅇ goes above the — on the left side of the syllable box and the ㅣ goes on the right side. Trace this syllable in different font styles and then practice on your own.

의	의	의	의	의					

 **Listen to the audio recording, repeat the letter and the words, then write the missing syllables.**

의사 **uisa** doctor

의	사		사

의자 **uija** chair

	자		자

2.1.5 Practice

Practice 1  Practice tracing and writing these syllables.

와	ㅇ	+	ㅗ	+	ㅏ	=	와	와				
외	ㅇ	+	ㅗ	+	ㅣ	=	외	외				
왜	ㅇ	+	ㅗ	+	ㅐ	=	왜	왜				
워	ㅇ	+	ㅜ	+	ㅓ	=	워	워				
웨	ㅇ	+	ㅜ	+	ㅔ	=	웨	웨				
위	ㅇ	+	ㅜ	+	ㅣ	=	위	위				
의	ㅇ	+	ㅡ	+	ㅣ	=	의	의				

Practice 2 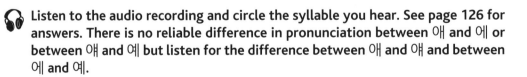 Listen to the audio recording and circle the syllable you hear. See page 126 for answers. There is no reliable difference in pronunciation between 애 and 에 or between 얘 and 예 but listen for the difference between 애 and 얘 and between 에 and 예.

1. 아   와   2. 어   워   3. 의   이

4. 왜   워   5. 웨   위   6. 외   의

Find some Korean text online and see if you can spot any **w**-based complex vowels. Compare different fonts. Are the ticks always parallel? Are they always the same length? Do they always touch the placeholder ○ or not touch it? Try imitating some of the font styles that you like best.

Practice 4 🎧 **Listen to the audio recording and fill in the blanks. See page 126 for answers.**

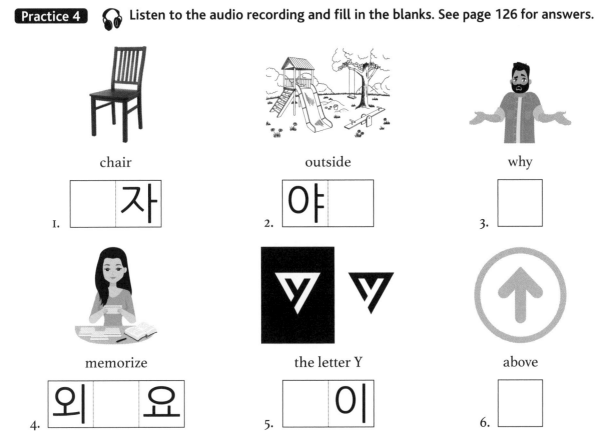

chair

outside

why

1. | | 자 | |

2. | 야 | |

3. | |

memorize

the letter Y

above

4. | 외 | | 요 |

5. | | 이 |

6. | |

2.1.6   All together!

Here are the sets of basic, **y**-based and **w**-based vowel syllables. Use the downloadable online flash cards to help you learn to distinguish syllables that look alike, such as 야 and 여. Don't forget about 의. It is not on the chart because it is neither **y**-based or **w**-based.

Basic vowel syllable	y-based complex vowel syllable	w-based complex vowel syllable
아	야	와
어	여	워
오	요	(no such vowel in Korean)
우	유	(no such vowel in Korean)
으	(no such vowel in Korean)	(no such vowel in Korean)
이	(no such vowel in Korean)	위 [wee] & 외 [weh]
애	얘	왜
에	예	웨

2.1.7 Practice

Practice 1 Practice reading these syllables. Listen to the audio to check your answers.

This exercise will help you recognize the difference between the basic vowel syllables 애 and 에 and their **y**-based counterparts, 얘 and 예, which are sometimes difficult to tell apart.

| kid | this kid | in; on; at | yes |
| 1. 애 | 2. 얘 | 3. 에 | 4. 예 |

Practice 2 Practice reading these syllables. Go back to page 37 if you need to check.

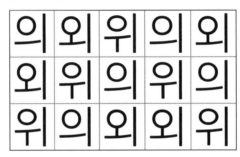

의 외 위 의 외
외 위 의 위 의
위 의 외 외 위

Practice 3 Fill in the blanks in the chart below. Refer to page 39 to check your answers.

Basic vowel syllable	y-based complex vowel syllable	w-based complex vowel syllable
아		
어		
오		(no such vowel in Korean)
우		(no such vowel in Korean)
으	(no such vowel in Korean)	(no such vowel in Korean)
이	(no such vowel in Korean)	____ [wee] & ____ [weh]
애		
에		

🎧 Practice reading these words aloud until you can read them smoothly. Use the audio recording to check your pronunciation. Then practice writing the words and develop your own handwriting style in Korean.

1. 아이   kid

아	이										

2. 오이   cucumber

오	이										

3. 우유   milk

우	유										

4. 위   above

위											

5. 왜   why

왜											

6. 이어요   connect

이	어	요						

7. 예의   manners

예	의							

8. 에이   the letter A

에	이							

9. 와이   the letter Y

와	이							

10. 우애   friendship, brotherly love

우	애							

3 CONSONANT SOUNDS AND LETTERS

Now we'll begin learning the consonant letters. As you are aware, consonant sounds are those that are made with parts of your mouth coming together and blocking some of the air that comes out of your mouth when talking. Sounds like the first ones in the words *cape*, *pie*, *cheese*, *zoo* and *nose* are all consonant sounds.

What you might not be immediately aware of is where in the mouth you make closure for each of those consonant sounds. But King Sejong was. He studied how the sounds are made and put his findings into the shapes of the consonant letters. This is why we can say that Hangul is very "scientific": it is based on King Sejong's studies of phonetics.

We'll explain some of that thinking along the way, but we will also offer useful images to help you remember the letters even without thinking about the phonetics.

Note that unlike Korean vowels, all Korean consonants have names. Their names are given at the beginning of each section, along with our own romanization aimed at helping you pronounce each letter name correctly.

To start off, we will go through the consonant letters one by one, learning the sounds they represent and key points about writing them. As Korean vowels and consonants are never written alone, only in syllables, we will practice writing each consonant in a syllable combination with the vowel ㅏ. When Korean initial consonants are paired with vowels, the consonants are written to the left of vertical vowels and above horizontal vowels.

Note that in this section of the book we present the consonant letters in a somewhat different order from traditional alphabetical order. This is to allow us to present the letters in order of complexity of their shape. For example, we present ㅁ and ㅂ before ㄴ, ㄷ and ㄹ, because it is a little easier to explain the reasoning behind the shape of the first two. And we present ㅎ right after ㅇ because ㅎ is derived from ㅇ.

3.1 Basic consonants

g, k

The first consonant in the Korean alphabet order is ㄱ. It represents a sound like **k** as in *hawk* or **g** as in *gaga*. It is made a little further back in the mouth than the **k** sounds in English words like *kiss* or *cap*, and it should not have a burst of air.

The name of this letter is 기역 [**gee-yuhk**].

The shape of the letter is meant to represent how its sound is made, with closure in the back part of the mouth, where your tonsils are located. You can remember this letter by imagining a baby saying "gaga."

gaga

To write ㄱ, make the horizontal stroke near the top of the syllable square and then make a vertical stroke downward. Make sure the strokes touch but do not extend past where they meet. The vertical stroke is usually longer than the horizontal stroke. Sometimes the lines are perpendicular, and sometimes the letter looks more like a handwritten "7," with a 45–60 degree angle.

This is considered one "stroke" in Hangul, like a 7, because you don't lift your pen.

We will practice this ㄱ consonant in a syllable.

The vertical stroke is often angled, like the numeral 7, depending on the font and letter combination. Trace this syllable in different font styles and then practice on your own.

🎧 Listen to the audio recording, repeat the syllable above and the words below, then practice reading and writing the words.

여가 leisure, spare time

아가 baby

ロ
m

How do you make a **mmm** sound as in *mom*? You have to bring your lips together and hum, right? The letter ㅁ that represents this sound is meant to show two parallel lips (top and bottom).

The name of this letter is 미음 [**mee-eum**].

To write ㅁ, make a short vertical stroke, top to bottom, on the left, then make a ㄱ or 7-shaped stroke from the top of the first line to form the top and right hand side, then make the bottom horizontal stroke. Be sure the lines all meet up at the corners and do not cross or go past the corners. The bottom line can be a little shorter than the top, but the letter should look like a box. To remember this letter, imagine lips about to say "mmmwah!"

mmmwah!

Be sure to follow the correct stroke order. We will practice this ㅁ consonant in a syllable.

ㅣ	ㄲ	ㅁ	ㅁ ㅁ	ㅁ + ㅏ = 아

The width of ㅁ is adjusted to make room for the ㅏ on the right. Trace this syllable in different font styles and then practice on your own.

마	마	마	마	마								

🎧 **Listen to the audio recording, repeat the syllable above and the words below, then practice reading and writing the words.**

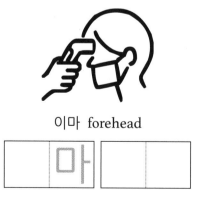

이마 forehead

마	

가마 traditional Korean palanquin

ㅂ
b, p

The letter ㅂ represents a sound like **p** as in *up-keep* or **b** as in *boy*. An English speaker can pronounce it like a **b** but be aware that it might sound like a **p** when a Korean speaker pronounces it. It is truly like a **p** but should not have a big burst of air after it (as the **p** does in *people* and *pie*).

> Have you heard of bibimbap? All of those lip sounds are ㅂ in Korean.

The name of this letter is 비읍 [**bee-eup**].

The shape of the letter is meant to resemble ㅁ, because the ㅂ sound is also made by putting the lips together. The idea is that ㅂ needs some extra lines to reflect that it has extra consonantness (or blocking of air). You can remember this letter by imagining it is a half-full mug of beer.

beer

The extra lines in writing ㅂ are not just added after making ㅁ, however. To write ㅂ, first make two parallel vertical strokes (left then right), then connect them with two horizontal ticks at the center and bottom. Make sure the strokes touch but do not extend past where they meet.

Be sure to follow the correct stroke order. We will practice this ㅂ consonant in a syllable.

ㅂ is made somewhat narrower to make room for a vowel to its right. Trace this syllable in different font styles and then practice on your own.

바	바	바	바	바							

🎧 **Listen to the audio recording, repeat the syllable above and the words below, then practice reading and writing the words.**

바나나 banana

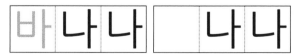

바위 rock

ㄴ
n

The letter ㄴ represents a sound like **n** as in *nose*. When you make an **n** sound, the tip of your tongue bends upwards to touch against the gums behind your upper teeth. That means that your tongue makes a ㄴ shape, right?

The name of this letter is 니은 [**nee-eun**].

Remember this letter by imagining the shape of a **kn**ee (wearing **ny**lon stockings). To write ㄴ, make a short vertical stroke downwards, then a slightly longer vertical stroke toward the right. You should not lift your pen between strokes. There should not be any overlap or gap between the strokes.

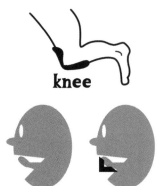

knee

Be sure to follow the correct stroke order. We will practice this ㄴ consonant in a syllable.

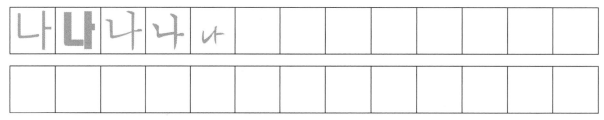

Notice that the ㄴ does not usually touch the ㅏ. Trace this syllable in different font styles and then practice on your own.

🎧 **Listen to the audio recording, repeat the syllable above and the words below, then practice reading and writing the words.**

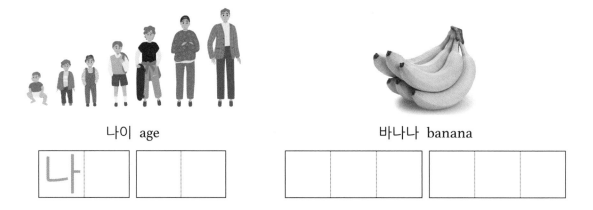

나이 age

바나나 banana

ㄷ

d, t

The letter ㄷ represents a sound like **t** as in *bet* or **d** as in *doe*. It sounds like the English **t** at times, but an English speaker is better off pronouncing it like a **d** to be sure that, like ㄱ and ㅂ, there is NO burst of air at the end of it.

The name of this letter is 디귿 [**dee-geut**].

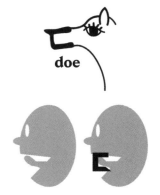

doe

To make a **t** or **d** sound, the tip of your tongue touches the gums behind your upper teeth, just like with ㄴ. When making **t** and **d**, the air is stopped completely: you can't hum a tune on just **t** or **d**, so ㄷ can be considered more consonant-like than ㄴ, and for this reason, King Sejong determined to add an extra stroke to ㄴ to make ㄷ.

To write ㄷ, make the top horizontal stroke first. Then make the ㄴ shape, meeting up with the top line. Be sure there isn't any overlap or gap between lines.

Be sure to follow the correct stroke order. We will practice this ㄷ consonant in a syllable.

Usually the ㄷ does not touch the ㅏ, especially not the top line, which is often just a bit shorter than the bottom line. Trace this syllable in different font styles and then practice on your own.

🎧 **Listen to the audio recording, repeat the syllable above and the words below, then practice reading and writing the words.**

바다 ocean, sea

다이아 diamond

ㄹ

l, r

When ㄹ is at the end of a syllable, it represents a sound like l in *limb*. It should always be a light l. When English speakers say "ball" or "bill," the l is pronounced partly in the throat. (This is sometimes called a "dark l.") That throat tightening should not happen when making a Korean end-of-syllable ㄹ. When ㄹ comes between vowels, it is pronounced with a Spanish or Japanese-like r sound, or the way American English speakers pronounce the t in *water* or the d in *ladder*. It is like l, but the tongue touches the gum ridge behind the teeth very quickly and lightly.

The name of this letter is 리을 [**lee-eul**].

When you make an l sound, the tip of your tongue touches the gums behind your upper teeth, like for ㄴ and ㄷ. ㄹ is in the group of tongue-tip sounds but while ㄹ is *less* consonant-like than ㄴ and ㄷ, it is still made by adding more lines to ㄷ.

You can remember this letter by imagining it is the shape of a ladder. To write ㄹ, make a small ㄱ shape (across and then down without lifting your pen), then the middle horizontal stroke left to right, then the ㄴ at the bottom. This letter is especially hard to write neatly, but try not to have any overlap or gap between lines.

LaDDeR

Be sure to follow the correct stroke order. We will practice this ㄹ consonant in a syllable.

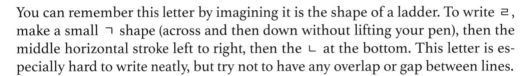

Notice that the ㄹ does not touch the ㅏ. Trace this syllable in different font styles and then practice on your own.

🎧 **Listen to the audio recording, repeat the syllable above and the words below, then practice reading and writing the words.**

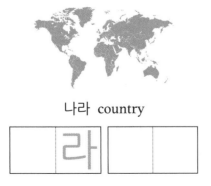

나라 country

라디오 radio

| | 라 | | | | 디 | | | 디 |

ㅅ
s

ㅅ represents a very soft, airy **s** sound, as in *kiss*. Imagine there is a **h** sound before and after the ㅅ, or that you are whispering. (There is another **s** sound in Korean that is "harder" or more hiss-like (see page 66), so you have to be extra careful that ㅅ sounds soft and airy.) Before ㅣ and before **y** sounds, however, ㅅ sounds like **sh** (as in *shell*), said while smiling and without sticking your lips out.

The name of this letter is 시옷 [**shee-oat**].

The shape of the letter can be seen as representing the teeth, seen from the side, because the air comes whispering out between your upper and lower teeth when you make this sound.

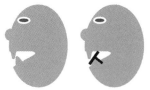

Remember this letter by imagining the soft whispering hiss of a saw, sawing wood, and the teeth of the saw looking like a row of ㅅㅅㅅ.

To write ㅅ, make an angled stroke, like a slash (/) but slightly curved. Then make the "kickstand" stroke, starting from the center point in the first line and going downwards at an angle. Make sure the lines touch but do not extend past where they meet.

saw-saw-saw

Be sure to follow the correct stroke order. We will practice this ㅅ consonant in a syllable.

  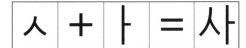

In some fonts and handwriting styles, the two angled strokes meet at the top, instead of at the center, and some fonts have curvier strokes than others. Trace this syllable in different font styles and then practice on your own.

사	**사**	사	사	사								

🎧 **Listen to the audio recording, repeat the syllable above and the words below, then practice reading and writing the words.**

사다 to buy

사	

이사 moving

ㅈ
j

ㅈ represents a **j** sound as in *juice* or a **ch** sound as in *each* but without a big burst of air afterwards. When Koreans start a word with this sound, it may sound like **ch** to you. But English speakers should probably imagine they are saying a soft, slightly airy or whispered **j** to make sure there is NO burst of air afterwards. This sound is also said while smiling without sticking your lips out.

The name of this letter is 지읒 [**jee-eut**].

> ㅈ is always pronounced **t** at the end of a syllable.

The shape of the letter ㅈ is intended to be like ㅅ with an added horizontal line at the top. That's because, instead of just a hissing sound like ㅅ, ㅈ is more consonant-like, with a hard stop at the beginning (like a **t** sound). To remember this letter, imagine a mouth with juice dribbling down the chin.

juice

To write ㅈ, make a horizontal top stroke, then the angled stroke and kickstand of ㅅ. Another way of thinking of it is, make a ㄱ with an angled stroke like a 7, then make the kickstand stroke, starting from the center point in the previous angled line and going downwards at an angle. Make sure the lines touch but do not extend past where they meet. In some fonts and handwriting styles, the angled stroke meets the top stroke at the center, instead of at the end like a ㄱ. Some fonts have more curvy angled strokes as well.

Be sure to follow the correct stroke order. We will practice this ㅈ consonant in a syllable.

Trace this syllable in different font styles and then practice on your own.

자 **자** 자 자 자

🎧 **Listen to the audio recording, repeat the syllable above and the words below, then practice reading and writing the words.**

자라 soft-shelled turtle

자

의자 chair

O

silent/ng

The letter ○ has two different functions. At the beginning of a syllable, ○ is a silent consonant, used as a placeholder at the beginning of a syllable that has no initial consonant sound. This is done because, in Hangul, each syllable block has to be written starting with a consonant *letter*. When ○ comes at the end of a syllable (see page 92), it is pronounced like the **ng** sound in *ring*.

The name of this letter is 이응 [**ee-eung**]. It contains both the silent and **ng** functions of ○.

When you make a **ng** sound, you close your throat (at the place where **k** and **g** are made). So the shape of the letter ○ is meant to resemble your throat as a hole. You can remember this letter by imagining your uvula as the ringer in a bell: ring-ng-ng-ng. (But at the beginning of a syllable, it is silent, like a bell unrung.)

ding-donnnng

To write ○, simply make a circle counterclockwise, starting at the top. How wide or narrow you make it depends on the other letters in the syllable block. Sometimes ○ is more oblong to make room for a vowel at the right.

Be sure to follow the correct stroke order. We will practice this ○ consonant in a syllable.

 or   ○ + ㅏ = 아

Trace this syllable in different font styles and then practice on your own.

아	아	아	아	아								

🎧 **Listen to the audio recording, repeat the syllable above and the words below, then practice reading and writing the words.**

아가 baby

아	

아마 maybe

ㅎ

h

The last basic consonant letter to learn is ㅎ, which represents the **h** sound in *hello*, *hamster* and *hat*. The shape of the letter is meant to be like ㅇ with extra lines on top because both sounds are made in the throat and ㅎ has more hissy air coming out, making it more consonant-like than (sing-song, hummable) ㅇ.

The name of this letter is 히읗, pronounced [**hee-eut**] because ㅎ is never pronounced as **h** at the end of a syllable, so in this case (at the very end), it is pronounced as **t**.

You can remember this letter because it looks a lot like a person wearing a hhhh-hat! To write ㅎ, make a short tick (horizontally), then a longer horizontal stroke under the first, then make a circle counterclockwise under the lines. Make sure the three strokes line up vertically and do not cross.

hat

Be sure to follow the correct stroke order.

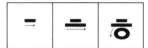

We will practice this ㅎ consonant in a syllable.

ㅎ + ㅏ = 하

Trace this syllable in different font styles and then practice on your own. Notice that some font styles have the first tick as a vertical line.

하	**하**	하	하	하							

 Listen to the audio recording, repeat the syllable above and the words below, then practice reading and writing the words.

하마 hippopotamus

하나 one

3.1.1 Review

Remember the relationships between the following pairs of letters? The one on the right adds a line or two as it is more consonant-like than the one on the left. The only basic consonant letter left out of this pattern is ㄱ.

ㅁ	ㅂ
ㄴ	ㄷ
ㅅ	ㅈ
ㅇ	ㅎ

(and then crazy ㄹ)

3.1.2 Practice

Practice 1 Practice reading the following syllables.

Practice 2 Practice reading the following words.

1. 사자   lion

2. 바다   sea

3. 아마   maybe

4. 하마   hippopotamus

5. 아가   baby

6. 의자   chair

7. 가사   lyrics

8. 하나   one

9. 나라   country, nation

Practice 3 Practice reading the following syllables in various fonts.

Practice 4 In the chart above, see how quickly you can find ...

3 **ga** syllables

2 **da** syllables

2 **ma** syllables

2 **ja** syllables

3 **ra** syllables

2 **ha** syllables

2 **na** syllables

2 **ba** syllables

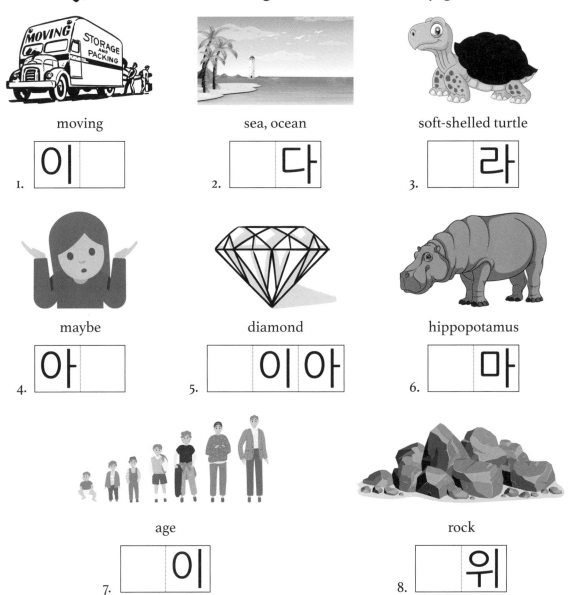

moving
1. 이[ ]

sea, ocean
2. [ ]다

soft-shelled turtle
3. [ ]라

maybe
4. 아[ ]

diamond
5. [ ]이아

hippopotamus
6. [ ]마

age
7. [ ]이

rock
8. [ ]위

3.2 Aspirated consonants

Now let's look at aspirated consonants. These consonants are based on five of the basic consonants you have learned already, but they are pronounced with an extra burst of air (that burst of air is called "aspiration.") Each aspirated consonant is formed by adding a single extra line to the basic consonant; this line can be considered as representing the extra burst of air.

ㅋ

k

You remember that ㄱ is like **k** as in *hawk* or **g** as in *gaga* and has no burst of air afterwards, right? When you add a horizontal stroke to make ㅋ, it represents the **k** sound in *king* and *cough* with a big burst of air after it. Think of saying "cough" while khhhhhoughing!

The name of this letter is 키역 [**khee-yuhk**].

> Note that ㅋ is pronounced ㄱ at the end of a syllable, with no burst of air.

To write ㅋ, make a ㄱ, then add a horizontal stroke that meets the vertical line at the center. Make sure the lines touch but do not extend past where they meet. The horizontal lines should be parallel.

To remember this letter, imagine someone *khhhhhoughing*, with extra "air" coming out of their mouth.

Be sure to follow the correct stroke order. We will practice this ㅋ consonant in a syllable.

c^hough!

The vertical stroke is often angled, like the numeral 7, depending on the font and letter combination. Trace this syllable in different font styles and then practice on your own.

🎧 **Listen to the audio recording, repeat the syllable above and the words below, then practice reading and writing the words.**

카카오 cacao

카드 card

ㅌ

t

The letter ㅌ represents a sound like **t** as in *time* or *attend*, with a big burst of air afterwards. Note that ㅌ is pronounced ㄷ at the end of a syllable.

The name of this letter is 티읕 [**thee-eut**].

The shape of the letter is meant to resemble ㄴ and ㄷ because like these two letters the ㅌ sound is also made by putting the tongue on the gums behind the top front teeth. The idea is that ㅌ adds one more horizontal line (compared to ㄷ) to reflect the extra burst of air. ㅌ is basically a ㄷ plus a horizontal line. Remember this letter by imagining it is the shape of a t^{hhh}oe, with a t^{hhh}oenail.

t^{h}oe

To write ㅌ, make ㄷ first, then add the extra horizontal stroke at the center. Be sure there isn't any overlap or gap between lines. We will practice this ㅌ consonant in a syllable.

Usually the ㅌ does not touch the ㅏ, especially not the top stroke, which is often just a bit shorter than the bottom. Trace this syllable in different font styles and then practice on your own.

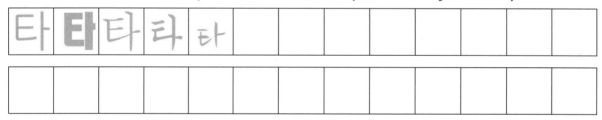

🎧 **Listen to the audio recording, repeat the syllable above and the words below, then practice reading and writing the words.**

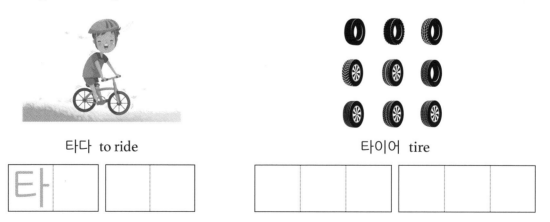

타다 to ride

타이어 tire

p

The letter ㅍ represents a sound like **p** as in *peek*, *pigeon* or *pop*, with a big burst of air after it. At the end of a syllable, ㅍ is pronounced as ㅂ, with no burst of air.

The name of this letter is 피읖 [**phee-eup**].

The shape of the letter is meant to resemble ㅁ and ㅂ because like these two letters the ㅍ sound is also made by putting the lips together. The idea is that ㅍ adds more horizontal lines (compared to ㅂ) to reflect the extra burst of air. (It turns out that the number of lines is the same, but the shape of ㅍ is more horizontally oriented.) You can remember this letter by imagining it is a window (with curtains,) and someone is sneakily p^hhheeking out.

p^heeking

To write ㅍ, first make a horizontal top stroke, then make two vertical ticks (left, then right). They may be parallel or closer at the bottom than at the top. Then finish it off with a bottom horizontal stroke. Make sure the lines touch but do not extend past where they meet. We will practice this ㅍ consonant in a syllable.

 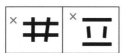

In some fonts and handwriting styles, the vertical ticks do not touch the top line. Trace this syllable in different font styles and then practice on your own.

🎧 **Listen to the audio recording, repeat the syllable above and the words below, then practice reading and writing the words.**

파 green onion

파마 perm

ch

The letter ㅊ represents a sound like **ch** as in *cheese* or *chime*, with a big burst of air afterwards. ㅊ is pronounced ㄷ at the end of a syllable, with no burst of air.

The name of this letter is 치읓 [**chee-eut**].

The shape of the letter is ㅈ with one more line added at the top (compared to ㅈ) to reflect the extra burst of air. You can remember this letter by imagining the extra air (and splatter) of "aa-chhhoooo!"

aa-chhhoo!

To write ㅊ, make the top tick first, then make a regular ㅈ, like a 7 followed by the right-hand leg. Be sure there isn't any overlap or gap between strokes. The tick stroke at the top may be horizontal, vertical or at a downwards angle—take your choice! We will practice this ㅊ consonant in a syllable.

Trace this syllable in different font styles and then practice on your own.

🎧 **Listen to the audio recording, repeat the syllable above and the words below, then practice reading and writing the words.**

차 car

마차 carriage

3.2.1 Review

Learning to hear and pronounce the difference between aspirated and basic consonants in Korean can be tricky. First review the letters and the intended pronunciation, and then just keep practicing your listening.

Practice 1 **Fill in the spaces in the chart with the basic or aspirated consonant letter to complete each pair. See page 126 for answers.**

ㄱ		ㅈ
	ㅌ	ㅍ

Practice 2 **Circle the consonants that are pronounced with a burst of air afterwards. See page 126 for answers.**

ㅊ　ㅂ　ㅍ　ㄷ　ㄴ　ㅇ　ㅁ　ㅌ　ㄹ　ㅋ　ㅈ

Practice 3 **Listen to the audio recording and fill in the blanks. See page 126 for answers.**

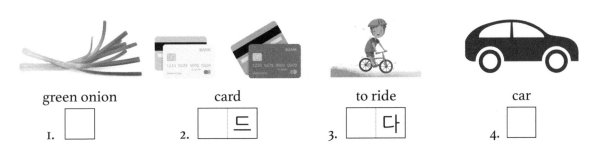

green onion	card	to ride	car
1. ☐	2. ☐ ㄷ	3. ☐ 다	4. ☐

3.2.2 Practice

Practice 1 **Practice writing all the consonants with the vowel ㅏ.**

1. 가

가																			

2. 나

나																			

3. 다

다																			

4. 라

| 라 | | | | | | | | | | | | | | | | | | | |

5. 마

| 마 | | | | | | | | | | | | | | | | | | | |

6. 바

| 바 | | | | | | | | | | | | | | | | | | | |

7. 사

| 사 | | | | | | | | | | | | | | | | | | | |

8. 아

| 아 | | | | | | | | | | | | | | | | | | | |

9. 자

| 자 | | | | | | | | | | | | | | | | | | | |

10. 차

| 차 | | | | | | | | | | | | | | | | | | | |

11. 카

| 카 | | | | | | | | | | | | | | | | | | | |

12. 타

| 타 | | | | | | | | | | | | | | | | | | | |

13. 파

| 파 | | | | | | | | | | | | | | | | | | | |

14. 하

| 하 | | | | | | | | | | | | | | | | | | | |

🎧 **Practice reading these words aloud until you can read them smoothly. Use the audio recording to check your pronunciation. Then practice writing the words.**

1. 가다   to go

가 다									

2. 사다   to buy

사 다									

3. 자다   to sleep

자 다									

4. 차다   to kick

차 다									

5. 타다   to ride

타 다									

6. 파다   to dig

파 다									

7. 하다   to do

하 다									

8. 나라   country

나 라									

9. 이마   forehead

이 마									

10. 카라   calla lily

카 라									

11. 의자   chair

의 자									

12. 하마   hippopotamus

하 마									

Practice 3 Listen to the audio recording and circle the syllable you hear. See page 126 for answers.

1. 가 　　 다 　　　　　 2. 나 　　 라

3. 마 　　 바 　　　　　 4. 아 　　 하

5. 가 　　 카 　　　　　 6. 다 　　 타

7. 자 　　 차 　　　　　 8. 바 　　 파

Practice 4 Listen to the audio recording and fill in the blanks. See page 126 for answers.

lion

1. 사 ☐

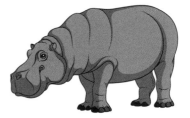

hippopotamus

2. 하 ☐

pie

3. ☐ 이

ocean, sea

4. ☐ 다

to buy

5. ☐ 다

to ride

6. ☐ 다

3.3 Tense or "twin" consonants

Tense or "twin" consonants are a very rare kind of sound among the world's languages, made with extra tensing of muscles in the throat (larynx). This tensing also leads to a higher pitch (high note, not yelling!) on the vowel that comes afterwards. They are written as a doubled-up version of a basic consonant, as you will see, and have no burst of air afterwards.

ㄲ

kk

The letter ㄲ is a doubled ㄱ. It represents a sound like a hard **g** when imitating the "kkaw kkaw" of a crow. There should be NO burst of air afterwards, so it is more like English **g** than English **k**. It is made a little further back in the mouth than the **g** sound in English as well.

The name of this letter is 쌍기역 [**ssahng-gee-yuhk**] which means "twin ㄱ."

To write ㄲ, make each of the two ㄱ a bit narrower, that is, with shorter horizontal strokes. This way, it looks like one (albeit complex) letter and takes up one letter's amount of space in the syllable box. This is especially important when there is a vertical vowel to the right. Be sure to make each half of the ㄲ separately, don't blend, cross or share lines.

kkaw-kkaw!

Be sure to follow the correct stroke order. We will practice this ㄲ consonant in a syllable.

Trace these syllables and then practice on your own.

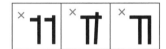

🎧 **Listen to the audio recording, repeat the syllable above and the words below, then practice reading and writing the words.**

아까 a while ago

까다 to peel

ㅃ

pp

The letter ㅃ is a doubled ㅂ. It represents a sound like a very pursed-lipped **b**. There should be NO burst of air afterwards, but extra tensing of the muscles in the throat, leading to a higher pitch on the following vowel. It might help to imagine tiny baby birds hungrily going "pbeep-peep."

The name of this letter is 쌍비읍 [**ssahng-bee-eup**] which means "twin ㅂ."

To write ㅃ, make each of the two ㅂ a bit narrower, that is, with shorter horizontal strokes. This way, it looks like one (albeit complex) letter and takes up one letter's amount of space in the syllable box. This is especially important when there is a vertical vowel to the right. Unlike most other letters, the center lines of the two ㅂ are shared in some font and handwriting styles.

pbeep-pbeep!

Be sure to follow the correct stroke order.

ㅣ	ㅣㅣ	ㅂ	ㅂ	ㅂㅣ	ㅂㅣㅣ	ㅂㅂ	ㅃ

We will practice this ㅃ consonant in a syllable.

ㅃ	+	ㅏ	=	빠

Trace these syllables and then practice on your own. You will find that in some fonts, the twin ㅂ share the center vertical line and even the horizontal lines!

빠	빠	빠	빠	빠							

🎧 **Listen to the audio recording, repeat the syllable above and the words below, then practice reading and writing the words.**

아빠 dad

빠	

오빠 older brother of female

ㄸ

tt

The letter ㄸ is a doubled ㄷ. It represents a sound like **d** when you press your tongue hard against the back of your upper teeth and say a very urgent "Ddang!" There should be NO burst of air afterwards, but extra tensing of the muscles in the throat, leading to a higher pitch on the following vowel.

The name of this letter is 쌍디귿 [**ssahng-dee-geut**] which means "twin ㄷ."

ddang!

To write ㄸ, make each of the two ㄷ a bit narrower, that is, with shorter horizontal strokes. This way, it looks like one letter. Unlike most other letters, the top lines of the two ㄷ are shared in some font and handwriting styles.

Be sure to follow the correct stroke order.

We will practice this ㄸ consonant in a syllable.

Trace these syllables and then practice on your own.

따	따	따	따	따								

🎧 **Listen to the audio recording, repeat the syllable above and the words below, then practice reading and writing the words.**

이따가 later

따다 to pick

ss

The letter ㅆ is a doubled ㅅ. It represents a sound like a very loud hissing. It is not usually much longer than the basic consonant ㅅ, but, in addition to the loud hissing, there is extra tensing of the muscles in the throat that leads to a higher pitch on the following vowel. This ㅆ is very SSaSSy!

The name of this letter is 쌍시옷 [**ssahng-shee-oht**] which means "twin ㅅ."

To write ㅆ, make each of the two ㅅ a bit narrower, and make the right leg of the left-hand ㅅ a little shorter, so that ㅅ can cuddle up to the right-hand ㅅ.

SSaSSy!

Be sure to follow the correct stroke order.

We will practice this ㅆ consonant in a syllable.

Trace these syllables and then practice on your own.

🎧 **Listen to the audio recording, repeat the syllable above and the words below, then practice reading and writing the words.**

싸다 to be cheap

비싸다 to be expensive

싸			

ㅉ

jj

The letter ㅉ is a doubled ㅈ. It represents a sound like a sudden, excited **dg** as in *edge* or **j** as in *jump*, where you get yourself ready in a **d** position, then suddenly burst out the **j** sound. There is extra tensing of the muscles in the throat as well, that leads to a higher pitch on the following vowel. It might help to think of this as a "tchoot-tchoo" (or "jjoo-jjoo") train whistle. NO burst of hissing air!

The name of this letter is 쌍지읒 [**ssahng-jee-eut**] which means "twin ㅈ."

To write ㅉ, make each of the two ㅈ a bit narrower, and the right leg of the left-hand ㅈ a little shorter, so that it can cuddle up to the right-hand ㅈ.

tchoot-tchoo!

Be sure to follow the correct stroke order.

We will practice this ㅉ consonant in a syllable.

ㅉ ＋ ㅏ ＝ 짜

Trace these syllables and then practice on your own.

🎧 **Listen to the audio recording, repeat the syllable above and the words below, then practice reading and writing the words.**

가짜 fake

	짜	

짜다 to be salty

3.3.1 Review

Practice 1 ✍️ Practice reading and writing these letters.

1. 까

| 까 | | | | | | | | | | | | | | | | | | | |

2. 따

| 따 | | | | | | | | | | | | | | | | | | | |

3. 빠

| 빠 | | | | | | | | | | | | | | | | | | | |

4. 싸

| 싸 | | | | | | | | | | | | | | | | | | | |

5. 짜

| 짜 | | | | | | | | | | | | | | | | | | | |

Practice 2 🎧 Practice reading these words aloud until you can read them smoothly. Use the audio recording to check your pronunciation. Then practice writing the words and develop your own handwriting style in Korean.

1. 까다   to peel

| 까 | 다 | | | | | | | | | | | | | | | | |

2. 따다   to pick

| 따 | 다 | | | | | | | | | | | | | | | | |

3. 싸다   to be cheap

| 싸 | 다 | | | | | | | | | | | | | | | | |

4. 짜다   to be salty

| 짜 | 다 | | | | | | | | | | | | | | | | |

5. 아빠   dad

| 아 | 빠 | | | | | | | | | | | | | | | | |

Practice 3 🎧 Listen to the audio recording and circle the syllable or word you hear. See page 127 for answers.

1. 까   따   2. 싸   짜

3. 가   까   4. 다   따

5. 아빠   아파   6. 차다   짜다

Practice 4 🎧 Listen to the audio recording and fill in the blanks. See page 127 for answers.

to be cheap

1. ☐ 다

to be salty

2. ☐ 다

to peel

3. ☐ 다

to pick

4. ☐ 다

dad

5. 아 ☐

fake

6. 가 ☐

3.3.2 Review

Let's review all of the "tense" or "twin" letters: ㄲ, ㄸ, ㅃ, ㅆ and ㅉ.

Practice 1 ✍ Complete the chart and practice pronouncing the three types of consonant in Korean. See page 127 for answers.

Basic/Plain	Aspirated (burst of air)	Tense
가		
	파	
		따
사	■	
	차	

3.3.3 All together!

These mnemonic images gather together the aspirated and tense consonant forms alongside their basic counterparts.

gaga

c\u02b0ough!

kkaw-kkaw!

doe

t\u02b0oe

ddang!

beer

p\u02b0eeking

pbeep-pbeep!

saw-saw-saw

SSaSSy!

juice

aa-chhhoo!

tchoot-tchoo!

3.3.4 Alphabetical order

These days, you can look up words in online dictionaries so the order of consonants and vowels may not seem critical for you to know, but it could come in handy for other kinds of ordering, and it is culturally relevant, too. (There are songs and chants, filing systems and other orderings that use the alphabet order, such as Exercise 가, Exercise 나, etc.).

The basic order is:

*Note that ㅇ here means words that start with a vowel sound. The vowel ordering is given below.

 Koreans often learn the order by chanting the syllables in groups of three and four, such as:

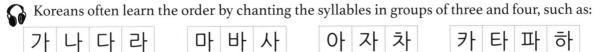

Beyond that, North and South Korean grammarians order the letters slightly differently, however. In South Korea, the double consonants come right after their corresponding basic letters in the dictionary reading order, while in North Korea, all double consonants come at the end, after all the basic letters.

South Korea:
ㄱ ㄲ ㄴ ㄷ ㄸ ㄹ ㅁ ㅂ ㅃ ㅅ ㅆ ㅇ ㅈ ㅉ ㅊ ㅋ ㅌ ㅍ ㅎ

North Korea:
ㄱ ㄴ ㄷ ㄹ ㅁ ㅂ ㅅ ㅈ ㅊ ㅋ ㅌ ㅍ ㅎ ㅇ ㄲ ㄸ ㅃ ㅆ ㅉ

*Note that ㅇ is ordered differently in North and South Korean alphabetical ordering.

There are some differences in how the two Koreas order the vowels as well. In South Korea, a basic vowel syllable like 아 comes before all of its variants like 애, 야 and 얘 before the next basic vowel syllable set begins; in North Korea, basic vowel syllables and their y-versions are given first, then 애 and 에 and their y-versions, followed by the w-versions of the vowels:

South Korea:
ㅏ ㅐ ㅑ ㅒ · ㅓ ㅔ ㅕ ㅖ · ㅗ ㅘ ㅙ ㅚ ㅛ · ㅜ ㅝ ㅞ ㅟ ㅠ · ㅡ ㅢ · ㅣ

North Korea:
ㅏ ㅑ ㅓ ㅕ · ㅗ ㅛ ㅜ ㅠ ㅡ ㅣ · ㅐ ㅒ ㅔ ㅖ · ㅚ ㅟ ㅢ ㅘ ㅝ ㅙ ㅞ

Here are the *letters* with their South Korean *names*. The irregular ones are highlighted. In North Korean, there are no irregular names: all consonant names have the same pattern.

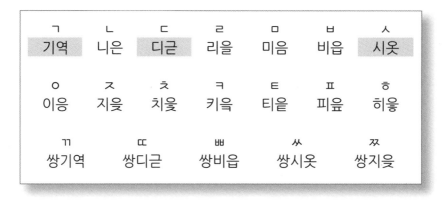

ㄱ	ㄴ	ㄷ	ㄹ	ㅁ	ㅂ	ㅅ
기역	니은	디귿	리을	미음	비읍	시옷

ㅇ	ㅈ	ㅊ	ㅋ	ㅌ	ㅍ	ㅎ
이응	지읒	치읓	키읔	티읕	피읖	히읗

ㄲ	ㄸ	ㅃ	ㅆ	ㅉ
쌍기역	쌍디귿	쌍비읍	쌍시옷	쌍지읒

4 READING AND WRITING HANGUL SYLLABLES

4.1 Letters into syllables

Korean letters are arranged into boxes that represent syllables. In Korean, *written* syllables can have a consonant followed by a vowel (CV), or consonant plus complex vowel (CVV), or C + V + a final consonant or two final consonants (CVC or CVCC).

4.2 Reading and writing CV syllables

You already know how to write a number of CV syllables in Korean. And you know that the initial consonant is written to the left of the vowel if the vowel has a long vertical stroke (or example, 가) and is written *above* the vowel if the vowel has a long horizontal stroke (for example, 오).

There are two shapes for CV syllables: the left-right kind used with vertical vowels and the top-bottom kind used with horizontal vowels. The table below shows some examples of the two basic CV syllable-box configurations:

CV	시 *poem*; 더 *more*; 자 *ruler*; 자다 *to sleep*; 새 *bird*; 새 *new*; 세 *three*; 네 *four*; 네 *yes*; 내 *my*
C⎵V	수 *number*; 조 *millet*; 효 *filial duty*; 오 *five*; 부모 *parents*; 도구 *tool*; 무모 *reckless*

Let's practice reading and writing each consonant paired with each vowel, starting with the vowels ㅏ and ㅓ. It will be good to practice writing and reading syllables with these two vowels at the same time so that your eyes get used to distinguishing them, and you don't confuse them.

These vowels also make for left-right syllable boxes. Since ㅏ and ㅓ have long vertical lines, the initial consonant will be written next to them, on the left, and it will be made a bit on the narrow side to share the syllable box left-and-right. That is, horizontal strokes will be made a little shorter.

Practice 1 Practice tracing and writing each consonant letter with the vowel ㅏ or ㅓ in the chart below.

가	ㄱ	+	ㅏ	=	가														
나	ㄴ	+	ㅏ	=	나														
다	ㄷ	+	ㅏ	=	다														
라	ㄹ	+	ㅏ	=	라														
마	ㅁ	+	ㅏ	=	마														
바	ㅂ	+	ㅏ	=	바														
사	ㅅ	+	ㅏ	=	사														
어	ㅇ	+	ㅓ	=	어														
저	ㅈ	+	ㅓ	=	저														
처	ㅊ	+	ㅓ	=	처														
커	ㅋ	+	ㅓ	=	커														
터	ㅌ	+	ㅓ	=	터														
퍼	ㅍ	+	ㅓ	=	퍼														
허	ㅎ	+	ㅓ	=	허														

Practice 2 🎧 Practice reading and writing these words.

사다 to buy

I.

사	다		

다리 leg

2.

다	리		

머리 head

3.

머	리		

허리 waist

4.

허	리		

Practice 3 **Practice reading and writing these letters.**

With the **y**-versions of the vowels ㅏ and ㅓ, namely ㅑ and ㅕ, the consonant also goes on the left side. Some of these syllables are very rare or do not occur at all in Korean words, but it is a clever and useful trait of Hangul that they *can* be written. That way Hangul can be used to write certain other-language syllables.

갸	ㄱ	+	ㅑ	=	갸													
냐	ㄴ	+	ㅑ	=	냐													
댜	ㄷ	+	ㅑ	=	댜													
랴	ㄹ	+	ㅑ	=	랴													
먀	ㅁ	+	ㅑ	=	먀													
뱌	ㅂ	+	ㅑ	=	뱌													
샤	ㅅ	+	ㅑ	=	샤													
여	ㅇ	+	ㅕ	=	여													
져	ㅈ	+	ㅕ	=	져													
쳐	ㅊ	+	ㅕ	=	쳐													
켜	ㅋ	+	ㅕ	=	켜													
텨	ㅌ	+	ㅕ	=	텨													
펴	ㅍ	+	ㅕ	=	펴													
혀	ㅎ	+	ㅕ	=	혀													

Practice 4 **Practice reading and writing these words.**

야구 baseball

1. | 야 | 구 | | |
|---|---|---|---|

샤워 shower

2. | 샤 | 워 | | |
|---|---|---|---|

티셔츠 T-shirt

3. | 티 | 셔 | 츠 | | |
|---|---|---|---|---|

쳐요 hit

4. | 쳐 | 요 | | |
|---|---|---|---|

Practice 5   Practice reading and writing these letters.

The vowels ㅗ and ㅜ have long horizontal strokes, so initial consonants go above these vowels.

> Notice how the vertical strokes of the consonants are shortened and often the C and V spaces overlap horizontally with the letters cuddling in together.

고	ㄱ	+	ㅗ	=	고								
노	ㄴ	+	ㅗ	=	노								
도	ㄷ	+	ㅗ	=	도								
로	ㄹ	+	ㅗ	=	로								
모	ㅁ	+	ㅗ	=	모								
보	ㅂ	+	ㅗ	=	보								
소	ㅅ	+	ㅗ	=	소								
우	ㅇ	+	ㅜ	=	우								
주	ㅈ	+	ㅜ	=	주								
추	ㅊ	+	ㅜ	=	추								
쿠	ㅋ	+	ㅜ	=	쿠								
투	ㅌ	+	ㅜ	=	투								
푸	ㅍ	+	ㅜ	=	푸								
후	ㅎ	+	ㅜ	=	후								

Practice 6   Practice reading and writing these words.

모자 hat

I. | 모 | 자 | | |
|---|---|---|---|

보다 to look

2. | 보 | 다 | | |
|---|---|---|---|

구두 dress shoes

3. | 구 | 두 | | |
|---|---|---|---|

두부 tofu

4. | 두 | 부 | | |
|---|---|---|---|

Letters and Syllables **75**

✍ **Practice reading and writing these letters.**

Syllables with ㅛ and ㅠ work just like those with ㅗ and ㅜ.

> Notice how the letters cuddle together and sometimes their lines touch.

교	ㄱ	+	ㅛ	=	교												
뇨	ㄴ	+	ㅛ	=	뇨												
됴	ㄷ	+	ㅛ	=	됴												
료	ㄹ	+	ㅛ	=	료												
묘	ㅁ	+	ㅛ	=	묘												
뵤	ㅂ	+	ㅛ	=	뵤												
쇼	ㅅ	+	ㅛ	=	쇼												
유	ㅇ	+	ㅠ	=	유												
쥬	ㅈ	+	ㅠ	=	쥬												
츄	ㅊ	+	ㅠ	=	츄												
큐	ㅋ	+	ㅠ	=	큐												
튜	ㅌ	+	ㅠ	=	튜												
퓨	ㅍ	+	ㅠ	=	퓨												
휴	ㅎ	+	ㅠ	=	휴												

🎧 **Practice reading and writing these words.**

도쿄 Tokyo

I. | 도 | 쿄 | | |

티켓 ticket

2. | 표 | |

리뷰 review

3. | 리 | 뷰 | | |

슈퍼 supermarket

4. | 슈 | 퍼 | | |

Practice 9 Practice reading and writing these letters.

Now try some syllables composed of C + — and C + | , thinking about how they are pronounced.

그	ㄱ	+	―	=	그											
느	ㄴ	+	―	=	느											
드	ㄷ	+	―	=	드											
르	ㄹ	+	―	=	르											
므	ㅁ	+	―	=	므											
브	ㅂ	+	―	=	브											
스	ㅅ	+	―	=	스											
이	ㅇ	+	|	=	이											
지	ㅈ	+	|	=	지											
치	ㅊ	+	|	=	치											
키	ㅋ	+	|	=	키											
티	ㅌ	+	|	=	티											
피	ㅍ	+	|	=	피											
히	ㅎ	+	|	=	히											

Practice 10 Practice reading and writing these words.

버스 bus

1. | 버 | 스 | | |

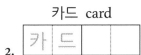

카드 card

2. | 카 | 드 | | |

치마 skirt

3. | 치 | 마 | | |

바지 pants

4. | 바 | 지 | | |

Practice 11 **Practice reading and writing these letters.**

Since ㅐ and ㅔ have long vertical lines, they go to the right of any initial consonant, making a left-right syllable box. Remember that ㅐ and ㅔ syllables sound the same in modern Korean.

개	ㄱ	+	ㅐ	=	개												
내	ㄴ	+	ㅐ	=	내												
대	ㄷ	+	ㅐ	=	대												
래	ㄹ	+	ㅐ	=	래												
매	ㅁ	+	ㅐ	=	매												
배	ㅂ	+	ㅐ	=	배												
새	ㅅ	+	ㅐ	=	새												
에	ㅇ	+	ㅔ	=	에												
제	ㅈ	+	ㅔ	=	제												
체	ㅊ	+	ㅔ	=	체												
케	ㅋ	+	ㅔ	=	케												
테	ㅌ	+	ㅔ	=	테												
페	ㅍ	+	ㅔ	=	페												
헤	ㅎ	+	ㅔ	=	헤												

Practice 12 **Practice reading and writing these words.**

개 dog

1. 개

게 crab

2. 게

배우 actor

3. 배 우

베개 pillow

4. 베 개

Practice reading and writing these letters.

The **y**-vowels, ㅐ and ㅖ are also vertical vowels, so the initial consonant goes on their left to make a left-right CV syllable box. Note that some syllables with ㅐ and ㅖ (e.g., 걔 and 계) sound very similar to their ㅐ or ㅔ counterparts.

개	ㄱ	+	ㅐ	=	개													
내	ㄴ	+	ㅐ	=	내													
새	ㅅ	+	ㅐ	=	새													
애	ㅇ	+	ㅐ	=	애													
재	ㅈ	+	ㅐ	=	재													
계	ㄱ	+	ㅖ	=	계													
례	ㄹ	+	ㅖ	=	례													
셰	ㅅ	+	ㅖ	=	셰													
예	ㅇ	+	ㅖ	=	예													
폐	ㅍ	+	ㅖ	=	폐													
혜	ㅎ	+	ㅖ	=	혜													

Practice 14 🎧 **Practice reading and writing these words.**

예의 manners

1. | 예 | 의 | | |

기계 machine

2. | 기 | 계 | | |

차례 order, turn

3. | 차 | 례 | | |

지폐 banknote, bill

4. | 지 | 폐 | | |

4.2.1 All together!

Practice 1 **Practice reading the syllables.** Try dropping a bean or bead onto the page and see how quickly you can read the syllable it lands on.

가	갸	거	겨	고	교	구	규	그	기
나	냐	너	녀	노	뇨	누	뉴	느	니
다	댜	더	뎌	도	됴	두	듀	드	디
라	랴	러	려	로	료	루	류	르	리
마	먀	머	며	모	묘	무	뮤	므	미
바	뱌	버	벼	보	뵤	부	뷰	브	비
사	샤	서	셔	소	쇼	수	슈	스	시
아	야	어	여	오	요	우	유	으	이
자	쟈	저	져	조	죠	주	쥬	즈	지
차	챠	처	쳐	초	쵸	추	츄	츠	치
카	캬	커	켜	코	쿄	쿠	큐	크	키
타	탸	터	텨	토	툐	투	튜	트	티
파	퍄	퍼	펴	포	표	푸	퓨	프	피
하	햐	허	혀	호	효	후	휴	흐	히

Practice 2 **Listen to the audio recording and circle the word you hear. See page 127 for answers.**

1. a. 소라 b. 수리   2. a. 야구 b. 여가   3. a. 어부 b. 여보   4. a. 예의 b. 애의

5. a. 가게 b. 거기   6. a. 누구 b. 노고   7. a. 보라 b. 부리   8. a. 슈퍼 b. 샤프

Practice 3 **Listen to the audio recording and fill in the blanks. Read each word out loud. See page 127 for answers.**

skirt

1. 치 | |

pants

2. 바 | |

hat

3. | 자 |

dress shoes

4. | 구 | | |

T-shirt

5. | 티 | | 츠 |

tomato

6. | | 마 | 토 |

cheese

7. | 치 | | |

pizza

8. | | 자 | |

spaghetti

9. | 파 | 게 | 티 |

cake

10. | 이 | 크 | |

Practice 4 🎧 Listen to the audio and find the city names, written horizontally, vertically or diagonally. The city names are on page 127 in the answers to Practice 5 .

시	구	마	유	패	토
자	카	르	타	하	쿄
도	레	고	라	노	시
제	주	시	파	이	조
네	마	드	리	드	누
바	미	니	혀	터	키

Practice 5 ✍ Write the word from the box above next to its English name. See page 127 for answers.

1. Chicago _____

2. Jeju _____

3. Paris _____

4. Tokyo _____

5. Hanoi _____

6. Geneva _____

7. Jakarta _____

8. Madrid _____

9. Sydney _____

4.3 Reading and writing CVV syllables

Another syllable shape in Korean is consonant plus complex vowel. This is known as a CVV syllable. You practiced how to make complex vowels in Section 2. You also practiced determining where the placeholder ○ goes in a syllable with no initial consonant sound. When there *is* a consonant sound at the beginning of a syllable with a complex vowel, the consonant goes in the same place as an initial ○ would, namely, on top of the horizontal vowel ㅗ, ㅜ or ―. That is, any initial consonant goes above the ㅗ or ㅜ that represents the **w** sound in a complex vowel syllable, or above the ― stroke of the complex vowel ㅢ.

 쇠 *iron*; 뇌 *brain*; 꾀 *artifice*; 꽤 *quite*; 죄 *sin, crime*; 왜 *why*; 쥐 *mouse*; 쏴 *shoot*; 뇌 *brain*

Let's practice the CVV syllables in smaller sets.

4.3.1 CVV syllables with ㅘ, ㅙ and ㅚ

Let's practice the CVV syllables that have ㅗ as the first vowel, representing the **w** sound. Any consonant can come before **w** + vowel in Hangul, though some of the syllables are rare or non-existent in Korean words. Can you read and pronounce all of them, nonetheless? Remember that ㅗ + ㅣ (ㅚ) is pronounced **weh**.

Practice 1   ✍ Practice reading and writing these letters.

Get used to distinguishing ㅗ + ㅏ from ㅗ + ㅣ.

과	ㄱ	+	ㅘ	=	과											
놔	ㄴ	+	ㅘ	=	놔											
봐	ㅂ	+	ㅘ	=	봐											
콰	ㅋ	+	ㅘ	=	콰											
화	ㅎ	+	ㅘ	=	화											
괘	ㄱ	+	ㅙ	=	괘											
돼	ㄷ	+	ㅙ	=	돼											
봬	ㅂ	+	ㅙ	=	봬											
쇄	ㅅ	+	ㅙ	=	쇄											
홰	ㅎ	+	ㅙ	=	홰											
괴	ㄱ	+	ㅚ	=	괴											
뇌	ㄴ	+	ㅚ	=	뇌											
뢰	ㄹ	+	ㅚ	=	뢰											

쇠	ㅅ	+	ㅚ	=	쇠										
최	ㅊ	+	ㅚ	=	최										

Practice 2 Practice reading and writing these words.

과자 cookies

1.
과	자		

최고 best

2.
최	고		

우뢰 thunder

3.
우	뢰		

돼지 pig

4.
돼	지		

4.3.2 CVV syllables with ㅝ, ㅞ, ㅟ and ㅢ

Now let's practice CVV syllables with ㅜ representing **w** combined with ㅓ-based vowels. Of course, it is possible to write any of these vowel combinations with any of the consonants before it, even if they don't all occur in Korean words. Remember that ㅜ + ㅣ (ㅟ) is pronounced **wee**.

Practice 1 Practice reading and writing these letters.

Get used to distinguishing ㅗ + ㅏ (in the previous section) from ㅜ + ㅓ.

궈	ㄱ	+	ㅝ	=	궈								
둬	ㄷ	+	ㅝ	=	둬								
뤄	ㄹ	+	ㅝ	=	뤄								
뭐	ㅁ	+	ㅝ	=	뭐								
줘	ㅈ	+	ㅝ	=	줘								
궤	ㄱ	+	ㅞ	=	궤								
쉐	ㅅ	+	ㅞ	=	쉐								
퀘	ㅋ	+	ㅞ	=	퀘								

훼	ㅎ	+	ㅞ	=	훼									
귀	ㄱ	+	ㅟ	=	귀									
뒤	ㄷ	+	ㅟ	=	뒤									
쉬	ㅅ	+	ㅟ	=	쉬									
취	ㅈ	+	ㅟ	=	취									
늬	ㄴ	+	ㅢ	=	늬									
의	ㅇ	+	ㅢ	=	의									
희	ㅎ	+	ㅢ	=	희									

Practice 2 Practice reading and writing these words.

뭐 what

1. | 뭐 | |
|---|---|

쥐요 give

2. | 쥐 | 요 | |
|---|---|---|

웨이터 waiter

3. | 웨 | 이 | 터 | | | |
|---|---|---|---|---|---|

쥐 mouse

4. | 쥐 | |
|---|---|

의사 doctor

5. | 의 | 사 | | |
|---|---|---|---|

희다 to be white

6. | 희 | 다 | | |
|---|---|---|---|

4.3.3 All together!

Practice 1 🎧 Listen to the audio recording and circle the syllable or word you hear. See page 127 for answers.

1. a. 죄   b. 쥐   2. a. 과자   b. 가자

3. a. 샤워   b. 사위   4. a. 우뢰   b. 의례

5. a. 쇠다   b. 쉬다   6. a. 봐요   b. 봬요

7. a. 돼지   b. 뒤주   8. a. 희다   b. 휘다

Practice 2 🎧 Listen to the audio recording and write the missing syllable. See page 127 for answers. Then read out each word.

apple

1. 사☐

pear

2. ☐

kiwi

3. 키☐

pig

4. ☐지

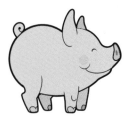

mouse

5. ☐

ant

6. ☐미

artist

7. ☐가☐

doctor

8. ☐사☐

actor

9. ☐우☐

4.4 Batchim and the Seven Representatives Rule

Hangul also allows for any consonant and even consonant pairs to be written at the end of a syllable. A consonant that comes at the end of a syllable is called a **batchim** [받침] and is written **at the bottom** of the syllable box, under any CV or CVV combination. A batchim may have one or two consonant letters.

Here are the resulting syllable shapes and some examples.

CV C	CV CC	달 *moon*; 빰 *cheeks*; 털 *body hair*; 형 *older brother*; 여덟 *eight*; 밝히다 *to brighten*; 삶다 *to boil*; 젊다 *to be young*
C V C	C V CC	몸 *body*; 죽 *gruel*; 꿈 *dream*; 물 *water*; 콩 *bean*; 굵다 *thick (girth)*; 옳다 *to be correct*; 끓다 *to boil (liquid)*
CV C		쾅 *boom, slam*; 뭘 *what*; 훨훨 *flap, flutter*; 꽉 *tight, full, fast*; 꿩 *pheasant*; 괄괄하다 *rough, tomboyish*

ㄸ, ㅃ and ㅉ don't happen to occur as batchim in Korean words

All single consonants can be batchim, but not all consonant pairs can. Even more importantly, not all consonants are pronounced the same at the end of a syllable as they are at the beginning. In fact, only seven consonant sounds, (ㄱ, ㄴ, ㄷ, ㄹ, ㅁ, ㅂ and ㅇ) known as the "Seven Representatives," can come at the end of the syllable. The reading and writing exercises that follow are grouped by batchim sound. First we'll study the single-consonant batchim and then we'll go on to practice batchim that are consonant pairs.

Practice 1   ✍ **Practice reading and writing these letters.**

The seven consonants below can be pronounced as expected in batchim position. Practice writing these "Seven Representatives" after 가, thinking about the pronunciation of each syllable as a whole.

각	가	+	ㄱ	=	각													
간	가	+	ㄴ	=	간													
갇	가	+	ㄷ	=	갇													
갈	가	+	ㄹ	=	갈													
감	가	+	ㅁ	=	감													
갑	가	+	ㅂ	=	갑													
강	가	+	ㅇ	=	강													

4.4.1 Final consonants ㄱ, ㅋ and ㄲ

Korean syllables end either with resonant sounds like ㅁ, ㄴ, ㄹ or the "neat," basic stopping sounds, ㄱ, ㄷ and ㅂ. Remember that ㅋ is a nearly identical twin to ㄱ, just pronounced with a big burst of air afterwards? And ㄲ is a an extra-tense ㄱ? In terms of mouth position, these three consonants are otherwise the same. So the representative sound for written ㅋ and ㄲ batchim is the closest basic stopping sound, ㄱ. That is, when ㅋ or ㄲ come at the end of a syllable, they are pronounced ㄱ (unless they can wrap into a following syllable that starts with a vowel. See The Spillover Rule, page 101).

Practice 1 Practice reading and writing these letters.

Keep in mind that all three batchim below are pronounced ㄱ.

박	바	+	ㄱ	=	박								
밖	바	+	ㄲ	=	밖								
억	어	+	ㄱ	=	억								
엌	어	+	ㅋ	=	엌								

Practice 2 🎧 Practice reading and writing these words with batchim pronounced as ㄱ.

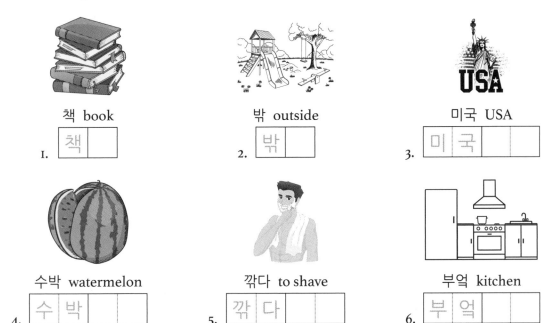

책 book
1. 책

밖 outside
2. 밖

미국 USA
3. 미 국

수박 watermelon
4. 수 박

깎다 to shave
5. 깎 다

부엌 kitchen
6. 부 엌

4.4.2 Final consonant ㄴ

ㄴ is one of the letters that can be pronounced as is when it is a batchim.

Practice 1   Practice reading and writing the syllable combinations in the chart below.

+	사	저	도	무	지	유	궈
ㄴ	산	전	돈	문	진	윤	권
ㄴ							

Practice 2   Practice reading and writing these words.

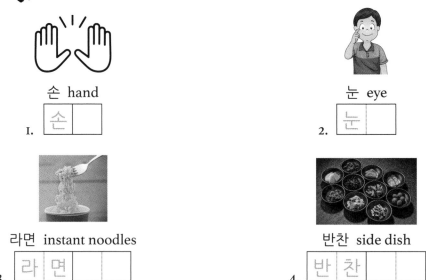

손 hand

1. 손

눈 eye

2. 눈

라면 instant noodles

3. 라 면

반찬 side dish

4. 반 찬

4.4.3 Final consonants ㄷ, ㅌ, ㅅ, ㅆ, ㅈ, ㅊ and ㅎ

ㄷ is one of the "Seven Representatives," meaning that it is one of the seven consonant sounds that can be used at the end of a syllable (remember that a consonant that comes at the end of a syllable is called a batchim). The consonant ㄸ happens to never occur as a batchim in written Korean words, but like the ㄱ, ㅋ, ㄲ set, ㄷ and ㅌ are also grouped together and pronounced as the basic consonant ㄷ when they are batchim. It may seem strange at first glance, but ㅈ, and ㅊ are also pronounced as ㄷ when they are batchim. (ㅉ happens to never occur as a batchim in Korean words.) When you pronounce these sounds, your tongue starts out in ㄷ position, in fact. In Korean, syllables end neatly, with no burst of air or continuation, so for ㅈ and ㅊ, we can only pronounce that first **t**-like part when they are batchim.

ㅅ and ㅆ also have a ㄷ representative pronunciation in batchim position. You can feel that ㅅ and ㅆ are pronounced with your tongue in almost the same place as for ㄷ if you try saying the last part of *cats*, or **t** followed rapidly by **s**.

The last member of the ㄷ representative batchim group is ㅎ. There isn't a logical phonetic reason for this. The consonant ㅎ [**h**] is nothing like ㄷ [**t/d**] phonetically. You just have to memorize this! The following practice exercises will help you get used to reading and writing syllables with ㄷ representative batchim pronunciation.

Practice 1 ✍ Practice writing the different batchim, remembering that all these are pronounced ㄷ.

낟	나	+	ㄷ	=	낟									
낫	나	+	ㅅ	=	낫									
낮	나	+	ㅈ	=	낮									
낯	나	+	ㅊ	=	낯									
낱	나	+	ㅌ	=	낱									
낳	나	+	ㅎ	=	낳									
났	나	+	ㅆ	=	났									

Practice 2 🎧 Practice reading and writing these words with the ㄷ-representative batchim.

듣다 to listen

1. | 듣 | 다 | | |

옷 clothes

2. | 옷 | |

있다 to exist

3. | 있 | 다 | | |

낮 daytime

4. | 낮 | |

솥 Korean traditional cauldron

5. | 솥 | |

꽃 flower

6. | 꽃 | |

 ㄱ ㄴ ㄷ
ㄹ ㅁ ㅂ ㅅ
ㅇ ㅈ ㅊ ㅋ
ㅌ ㅍ ㅎ ♡

히읗 name of the Korean letter ㅎ

7. | 히 | 읗 | | |

꽃 light

빛 light

8. | 빛 | |

4.4.4 Final consonant ㄹ

ㄹ is one of the "Seven Representatives," or consonants that can be pronounced in the batchim position BUT it is pronounced slightly differently as a batchim than at the beginning of a syllable. At the beginning of a syllable, ㄹ is pronounced like the Spanish or Japanese **r** in words like *cara* (Spanish for "face") and *pera-pera* (Japanese for "fluent"). When it is a batchim, it sounds like the clear **l** in English words like *lily* and *lake*. It is not a dark **l** as in the words *ball*, *bulk* and *toll*. You should not feel a closing or tightness in your throat when you make the ㄹ batchim sound. Try smiling when you make this sound to be sure you don't make it dark and throaty.

Practice 1 Practice reading and writing the syllable combinations in the chart below. Notice that the letters all get flattened a bit to fit in the box. Try saying them with a light l sound.

+	다	퍼	보	수	느	규	워
ㄹ	달	펄	볼	술	늘	귤	월
ㄹ							

Practice 2 Practice reading and writing these words with the ㄹ batchim.

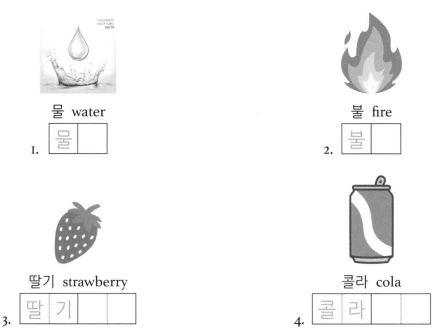

물 water
I. 물

불 fire
2. 불

딸기 strawberry
3. 딸 기

콜라 cola
4. 콜 라

4.4.5 Final consonant ㅁ

ㅁ can also be pronounced as is in batchim position. (You might have noticed that the resonant sounds like ㅁ, ㄴ and ㄹ work fine as batchim while the harder consonants get "reduced" to a basic stopping sound.

✍ Practice reading and writing the syllable combinations in the chart below. It's fun to practice fitting the different letter shapes into a syllable box!

+	사	저	보	수	기	냐	과
ㅁ	삼	점	봄	숨	김	냠	괌
ㅁ							

Practice 2 🎧 Practice reading and writing these words with the ㅁ batchim.

밤 night

I. 밤

잠 sleeping

2. 잠

구름 cloud

3. 구 름

바람 wind

4. 바 람

4.4.6 Final consonants ㅂ and ㅍ

The aspirated consonant ㅍ has a burst of air afterwards, but ㅂ does not, so ㅂ and ㅍ are both pronounced as ㅂ when they are batchim. And ㅃ happens to never occur as a batchim in Korean words. It turns out then, that some sets of words are pronounced the same even though they are spelled differently, for example, those with ㅂ versus ㅍ as batchim.

Practice 1 ✍ Practice reading and writing these syllables with ㅂ or ㅍ as batchim.

입	이	+	ㅂ	=	입											
잎	이	+	ㅍ	=	잎											
섭	서	+	ㅂ	=	섭											
섶	서	+	ㅍ	=	섶											

집 house

I. 집

숲 forest

2. 숲

잎 leaf

3. 잎

입 mouth

4. 입

4.4.7   Final consonant ㅇ

The last single-consonant batchim to talk about is ㅇ. You remember that ㅇ is not pronounced when it comes at the beginning of a syllable before the vowel, such as in 아 and 입. How is ㅇ pronounced when it is a batchim? In this position it is like the **ng** in *ring* and *sing*. And since it is a resonant sound, it is one of the seven possible batchim sounds. Let your ㅇ ring out at the end of these syllables as you practice reading and writing!

Practice 1 Practice reading and writing the syllable combinations in the chart below.

+	가	서	조	구	리	녀	와
ㅇ	강	성	종	궁	링	녕	왕
ㅇ							

Practice 2 Practice reading and writing these words with the ㅇ batchim.

강 river

I. 강

왕 king

2. 왕

등산 hiking

3.
등	산		

영화 movie

4.
영	화		

4.4.8   CC batchim

There are some two-consonant batchim that occur in the spelling of Korean words, but only one of those two consonants is ever pronounced when the next syllable starts with a consonant. If the next syllable starts with a vowel, the second batchim consonant can be pronounced as part of the next syllable (see The Spillover Rule on page 101 for more).

As you can see in the following examples of two-consonant batchim, the two-consonant letters are simply written next to each other under the CV beginning of the syllable. The chart also shows how each particular CC batchim is pronounced along with example words.

Batchim	Pronunciation	Examples [pronunciation]	Meaning
ㄳ	ㄱ	몫 [목]	a share, quotient
ㄵ	ㄴ	앉다 [안따]	to sit
ㄶ	ㄴ	많다 [만타]	a lot
ㄺ	ㄹ / ㄱ	읽고 [일꼬]	read-and
ㄻ	ㄹ / ㅁ	삶다 [삼따]	to boil
ㄼ	ㄹ	여덟 [여덜]	eight
ㄽ	ㄹ	외곬 [외골]	inflexible-minded
ㄾ	ㄹ	핥다 [할따]	to lick
ㄿ	ㄹ / ㅂ	읊다 [읍따]	to recite
ㅀ	ㄹ	앓다 [알타]	to suffer
ㅄ	ㅂ	값 [갑]	price

Practice 1 Practice reading and writing the following CVCC syllables.

넋	너	+	ㄳ	=	넋										
몫	모	+	ㄳ	=	몫										
앉	아	+	ㄵ	=	앉										
엱	어	+	ㄵ	=	엱										
많	마	+	ㄶ	=	많										
찮	차	+	ㄶ	=	찮										

닭	다	+	ㄺ	=	닭										
읽	이	+	ㄺ	=	읽										
삶	사	+	ㄻ	=	삶										
앎	아	+	ㄻ	=	앎										
덟	더	+	ㄼ	=	덟										

짧	짜	+	ㄼ	=	짧										
곬	고	+	ㄽ	=	곬										
핥	하	+	ㄾ	=	핥										
읖	으	+	ㄿ	=	읖										

끊	끄	+	ㅀ	=	끊										
앓	아	+	ㅀ	=	앓										
값	가	+	ㅄ	=	값										
없	어	+	ㅄ	=	없										

Practice 2 Practice reading and writing these words with two-consonant batchim.

값 price

I. 값 [ ]

life is good

삶 life

2. 삶 [ ]

여덟 eight

3.  | 여 | 덟 | | |

읽다 to read

4. | 읽 | 다 | | |

괜찮다 to be okay

5. | 괜 | 찮 | 다 | | |

끓다 to boil

6. | 끓 | 다 | | |

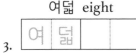

핥다 to lick

7. | 핥 | 다 | | |

앉다 to sit down

8. | 앉 | 다 | | |

4.4.9 All together!

Wow! You've made it through all the vowels and vowel combos, all the consonants and all the syllable types (CV, CVV, CVC and CVCC). Keep practicing reading and writing, even words you do not know. Start by identifying the individual letters, then practice reading a whole syllable at a time. Little by little you will build your reading speed and reflexive reading. *You're off!*

Practice 1 Listen to the audio and circle the syllable you hear. See page 127 for answers.

1. a. 강　　　 b. 감　　　　　　　2. a. 산　　　 b. 살

3. a. 잠　　　 b. 장　　　　　　　4. a. 박　　　 b. 밭

5. a. 빛　　　 b. 빕　　　　　　　6. a. 넗　　　 b. 넉

7. a. 짚　　　 b. 짐　　　　　　　8. a. 숫　　　 b. 숲

Practice 2　Choose the syllable that is pronounced differently from the others. See page 127 for answers.

1. a. 잎　　 b. 입　　 c. 임　　　　2. a. 업　　 b. 억　　 c. 엌

3. a. 솥　　 b. 솝　　 c. 솟　　　　4. a. 각　　 b. 갓　　 c. 갇

Practice 3   Practice reading these words aloud until you can read them smoothly. Use the audio recording to check your pronunciation. Then practice writing the words and develop your own handwriting style in Korean.

Fruit (과일)

1. 사과   apple

사 과										

2. 오렌지   orange

오 렌 지							

3. 포도   grape

포 도										

4. 딸기   strawberry

딸 기										

5. 레몬   lemon

레 몬										

6. 파인애플   pineapple

파 인 애 플					

7. 배   pear

배											

8. 바나나   banana

바 나 나								

9. 키위   kiwi

키 위										

10. 복숭아   peach

복 숭 아								

11. 체리   cherry

체 리										

12. 감   persimmon

| 감 | | | | | | | | | | | | | | | | |

13. 참외   Korean honeydew-like melon

| 참 | 외 | | | | | | | | | | | | | | | |

14. 수박   watermelon

| 수 | 박 | | | | | | | | | | | | | | | |

Animals (동물)

1. 개   dog

| 개 | | | | | | | | | | | | | | | | |

2. 고양이   cat

| 고 | 양 | 이 | | | | | | | | | | |

3. 말   horse

| 말 | | | | | | | | | | | | | | | | |

4. 양   sheep

| 양 | | | | | | | | | | | | | | | | |

5. 오리   duck

| 오 | 리 | | | | | | | | | | | | | | | |

6. 닭   chicken

| 닭 | | | | | | | | | | | | | | | | |

7. 돼지   pig

| 돼 | 지 | | | | | | | | | | | | | | | |

8. 소   cow

| 소 | | | | | | | | | | | | | | | | |

9. 토끼   rabbit

| 토 | 끼 | | | | | | | | | | | | | | | |

SECTION TWO

SAY IT LIKE A KOREAN!

5   BASIC PRONUNCIATION RULES

The Korean alphabet has one way to spell each sound. Only one sound is represented by each letter (unlike English: _phone_, _fish_). Hangul never requires multiple letters to spell a single sound either (unlike English: _catch_, _bridge_). So it is a fairly simple system. To master correct _pronunciation_ of Korean spelling, however, there are certain principles or "rules" to learn, which will improve your understanding, spelling and pronunciation.

Note that in all the examples given in this section, the pronunciation of a word is given in brackets.

5.1   The "Seven Representatives" Rule

☞ **Only seven batchim can be pronounced as spelled.**
As we mentioned in section 4.4, a consonant or consonant pair that comes at the end of a syllable it is called a batchim. Only seven batchim can be pronounced as spelled (if a vowel doesn't follow): the four resonant sounds, ㄴ, ㄹ, ㅁ and ㅇ, and three basic, stopping consonants ㄱ, ㄷ and ㅂ. These seven batchim are often referred to as the "Seven Representatives."

5.1.1   🎧 Final consonants ㄴ, ㅁ, ㅇ and ㄹ

If the final consonant of the word is one of the resonant sounds ㄴ, ㅁ, ㅇ or ㄹ, you can say it as is.

돈 _money_   삼 _three_   강 _river_   발 _foot_

If the final consonant is other than ㄴ, ㅁ, ㅇ or ㄹ, you pronounce it as one of the three kinds of basic, stopping consonants, ㄱ, ㄷ or ㅂ, as explained in the following sections.

5.1.2   🎧 The ㄱ kind

When the consonants ㄱ, ㄲ, ㄳ or ㅋ appear at the end of a syllable, they are pronounced as ㄱ when no vowel follows.

박	[박]	_Park (Korean last name)_
밖	[박]	_outside_
몫	[목]	_(one's) share_
부엌	[부억]	_kitchen_

5.1.3   🎧 The ㅂ kind

When the consonants ㅂ, ㅄ or ㅍ (all sounds you make with the lips together) appear at the end of a syllable, they are pronounced as ㅂ when no vowel follows.

집	[집]	_house_
값	[갑]	_price_
짚	[집]	_straw_

5.1.4 🎧 The ㄷ kind

When the tongue-tip consonants ㄷ, ㅅ, ㅆ, ㅈ, ㅊ, ㅌ or ㄸ appear at the end of a syllable, they are pronounced as ㄷ when no vowel follows. That means you sometimes run into sets of homophones (words that sound alike but are spelled differently), as in these examples:

낟	[낟]	*grain*
낫	[낟]	*sickle*
낮	[낟]	*daytime*
낱	[낟]	*each piece*
났	[낟]	*came to be*
낯	[낟]	*face (older usage)*

Basically, Korean does NOT pronounce sounds like **s** or **ch** at the end of a word, even if the word is spelled that way. This is partly why words from other languages change in pronunciation when borrowed into Korean, often by adding vowels.

bus 버스   *yes* 예스   *bench* 벤치

For related reasons, borrowed words with a final **t** are written with a ㅅ:

racket 라켓   *Elliot* 엘리엇   *Camelot* 카멜롯

5.2 🎧 The Spillover Rule

☞ **A batchim consonant spills over to the next syllable if that syllable begins with a vowel (signaled by a written ㅇ).**

So, for example, the batchim ㄲ in 밖 meaning *the outside* is pronounced as ㄱ when the word is said alone, according to the Seven Representatives Rule. But the Spillover Rule says that when a particle beginning with a vowel sound, such as 에, meaning *in/at/on*, is added after it (as in 밖에 meaning *on the outside*), the batchim ㄲ is pronounced as the beginning of that next syllable. It can also be pronounced with its original tense consonant pronunciation. It sounds like [바께]. It is important to remember, however, that a batchim consonant does not move to the beginning of the syllable *in the spelling*.

Below are some more examples. In the left-hand columns, we see the Seven Representatives Rule affecting the pronunciation of the word, and in the right-hand columns, we see the Spillover Rule affecting it. Notice that the *spelling* of the main word is the same whichever pronunciation rule might be at play.

Spelling	Seven Reps Pronunciation	Meaning	Spelling	Spillover Pronunciation	Meaning
밖	[박]	*the outside*	밖에	[바께]	*on the outside*
부엌	[부억]	*kitchen*	부엌에	[부어케]	*in the kitchen*
낫	[낟]	*sickle*	낫을	[나슬]	*sickle + direct object marker*
입	[입]	*mouth*	입이	[이비]	*mouth + subject marker*
앞	[압]	*front*	앞에	[아페]	*in front of*

If the batchim has two consonants, only the second consonant spills over.

Spelling	Seven Reps Pronunciation	Meaning	Spelling	Spillover Pronunciation	Meaning
읽	[익]	to read	읽을	[일글]	read (imperfect/future)
앉	[안]	to sit	앉아	[안자]	(someone) sits
밟	[발, 밟]	to step on	밟으면	[발브면]	if (someone) steps on
값	[갑]	price	값을	[갑쓸]	price + direct object marker

> The use of ㅆ instead of ㅅ here is explained at the end of this section.

The Spillover Rule can help you determine how a final consonant should be written. Though the final batchim gets reduced due to the Seven Representatives Rule, and you cannot determine how to spell the word when it is said alone, the "true identity" of a letter is revealed by the Spillover Rule when particles and suffixes are added:

앞 [압] *front*   BUT   앞으로 [아프로] *toward the front/in the future*
값 [갑] *price*   BUT   값을 [갑쓸] *price (object of verb)*

Referring to the homophones we mentioned earlier, look what happens when a syllable starting with a vowel is added to the word. In the gray right-hand columns in the table below, we see that the Spillover Rule provides a context in which you can *hear* what the batchim consonant really is.

Spelling	Pronunciation	Meaning	Spelling	Pronunciation	Meaning
낟	[낟]	grain	낟에	[나데]	on the grain
낫	[낟]	sickle	낫에	[나세]	on the sickle
낮	[낟]	daytime	낮에	[나제]	in the daytime
낱	[낟]	each piece	낱에	[나테]	on each piece
났	[낟]	come to be	났어	[나써]	come to be
낯	[낟]	face (older usage)	낯에	[나체]	on the face

5.3 🎧 Double final-consonant reduction

When there are two consonants in the batchim (and no vowel follows), sometimes only one of them is pronounced. When there is a following consonant, it often becomes tense (see section 5.6.4). This happens often when suffixes such as 고 meaning *and* are added. We offer some guidelines here, but note that everyday pronunciation as well as official standards do change, and some speakers may pronounce these syllables differently.

☞ **The FIRST consonant is pronounced when the second is ㅅ or ㅈ**

There are four possible batchim clusters for this case: ㄳ, ㅄ, ㄵ, ㄼ.

몫   [목]   *share*
앉고   [안꼬]   *sit-and*
외곬   [외골]   *single-minded*
값   [갑]   *cost, price*

☞ When ㄹ is the first consonant in a double-consonant batchim, pronunciation varies widely among speakers.

핥고	[할꼬]	lick-and*
읽고	[일꼬] or [익꼬]	read-and
밟고	[발꼬] or [밥꼬]	step on-and
맑다	[맑따] or [막따] or [말따]	to be clear (skies)

*Note that tongue-tip sounds like ㅌ are most likely to go unpronounced.

☞ Pronunciation is arbitrarily fixed in these words:

닭	[닥]	chicken
여덟	[여덜]	eight
삶고	[삼꼬]	boil (of food in liquid)-and

5.4 🎧 Vowel simplification

Korean complex vowel syllables that contain **w** and **y** sounds are often simplified in natural, casual speech. The spelling does not change. (This also means you need to pay attention to homophones: words that are pronounced the same but spelled differently.)

☞ ㅕ is pronounced as [ㅓ] after ㅈ, ㅉ, ㅊ (but not after ㅅ)

Pronounce 마셔 *drink* as expected but:

가져	[가저]	have
쪄	[쩌]	steam
다쳐	[다처]	get hurt

☞ ㅖ is pronounced as [ㅔ] after a consonant

Pronounce 예보 *weather forecast* as expected but:

시계	[시게]	clock
계산서	[게산서]	bill
실례합니다	[실레암니다]	excuse me
안녕히 계세요	[안녕이 게세요]	goodbye

☞ ㅘ and ㅙ are pronounced [ㅏ] or [ㅐ] after a consonant, with a hint of **w** added onto the consonant:

Pronounce 이리 와 *Come here!* as expected but:

안 돼	[안 **W**대]	No way!
놔요	[**W**나요]	let go
전화번호	[저 **W**나버노]	phone number
괜찮아	[**W**갠차나]	it's ok
봤어?	[**W**받써] or [**W**바써]	Did you see?

☞ ㅝ and ㅚ **are pronounced [ㅓ] , [ㅗ] or [ㅔ] after a consonant, with a hint of w added onto the consonant**

Pronounce 워싱턴 *Washington* as expected but:

뭐	[ᵂ머 or ᵂ모]	*what*
줘요	[ᵂ저요 or ᵂ조요]	*give*
관둬	[ᵂ곤 ᵂ도 or ᵂ간 ᵂ도 or ᵂ간 ᵂ더]	*forget it*
처음 뵙겠어요	[처음 ᵂ베께써요]	*nice to meet you*

5.5 🎧 The single-spelling principle

A main guiding principle of Korean spelling is that each word or part of a word (that is, a root or a suffix, for example), is spelled the same way regardless of how pronunciation rules have changed its pronunciation. (It's the same in English where we spell *compet-* the same way, even though it is pronounced differently in *compete* and *competition*.) So, since the root word for *eat* is 먹 , it is spelled the same way regardless of what suffix is attached or how the pronunciation changes:

Spelling	Pronunciation	Meaning
먹지?	[먹찌]	*Eating, right?*
먹어요	[머거요]	*eats, is eating* (present polite form)
먹는다	[멍는다]	*I'm eating this.* (intimate/written style)
먹고 가	[먹꼬 가]	*eat and then go*

So, the good speller's rule of thumb is: "Don't just write what you hear; think about the root word and what it is joining with when you are writing."

5.6 Interactions between consonants

As well as the basic rules above, there are a few cases of consonant-consonant interactions that result in pronunciations that don't resemble a word's spelling. That is, when certain consonants are next to each other, they interact and result in a new and somewhat unexpected pronunciation. They make sense though, so you can get the hang of them with practice. You may even realize you have done some of these pronunciation changes without thinking.

5.6.1 🎧 Aspiration

ㅎ combines with a basic consonant before or after it to yield a consonant with a big burst of air (ㅋ, ㅌ, ㅍ or ㅊ):

ㄱ + ㅎ = [ㅋ]	ㅎ + ㄱ = [ㅋ]
백화점 [배콰점]	어떻게 [어떠케]
department store	*how*

ㄱ + ㅎ = [ㅋ]	ㅎ + ㄱ = [ㅋ]

착해 [차캐]
good, mild-mannered

좋고 [조코]
good and

ㄷ + ㅎ = [ㅌ]	ㅎ + ㄷ = [ㅌ]

맏형 [마텽]
the eldest brother

많다 [만타]
tons

비슷해요 [비스태요]
similar

넣든지 [너튼지]
put in or...

ㅅ + ㅎ = [ㅌ]	ㅎ + ㅈ = [ㅊ]

못 해요 [모태요]
can't do

그렇지만 [그러치만]
but

옷하고 [오타고]
clothes and

괜찮지 [괜찬치 or ᵂ 갠찬치]
ok, right?

ㅂ + ㅎ = [ㅍ]

법학 [버팍]
study of law

답답해 [답따패]
frustrated, stir-crazy

5.6.2 🎧 Nasalization

A consonant right before one of the nasal consonants ㄴ or ㅁ is pronounced as a nasal.

☞ ㄱ, ㅋ and ㄲ become ㅇ

먹는	[멍는]	*eating*	학년	[항년]	*school year*
백년	[뱅년]	*100 years*	섞는	[성는]	*mixing*
부엌만	[부엉만]	*kitchen only*	한국말	[한궁말]	*the Korean language*

☞ ㅂ, ㅍ and ㅃ become ㅁ

십만	[심만]	*hundred thousand*	앞문	[암문]	*front gate*
앞날	[암날]	*future*	합니다	[함니다]	*does/do*
없네	[엄네]	*not there*	급모	[금모]	*urgent recruiting*

☞ ㄷ, ㅌ, ㄸ, ㅅ, ㅆ, ㅈ, ㅊ and ㅉ become ㄴ

있니?	[인니]	*Is there?*
끝나다	[끈나다]	*to end*
꽃망울	[꼰망울]	*flower bud*
못 먹어	[몬머거]	*cannot eat*
웃네	[운네]	*smiling*
낱말	[난말]	*word, vocabulary*
잇몸	[인몸]	*gums*
뒷머리	[뒨머리]	*hair in the back (not the bangs)*
웃는 사람	[운는 사람]	*a laughing/smiling person*

5.6.3 🎧 ㄹ beats ㄴ

When a ㄴ meets a ㄹ (in either order), the sequence is pronounced as ㄹㄹ:

👉 ㄴ + ㄹ = [ㄹㄹ]

신라	[실라]	*Silla Kingdom*	한라산	[할라산]	*Mt. Halla*
연락	[열락]	*contact, call*	편리	[펼리]	*convenience*
관리	[괄리]	*management*	곤란	[골란]	*difficulty*

👉 ㄹ + ㄴ = [ㄹㄹ]

달님	[달림]	*moon (honorific)*	칼날	[칼랄]	*blade of a knife*
월남	[월람]	*Vietnam*	물난리	[물랄리]	*flood*
실내	[실래]	*inside*	발냄새	[발램새]	*stinky feet smell*

📌 **Hint for reading**

As the previous sections show, learning how to read words (out loud) correctly involves looking at least one syllable ahead. In words like 신라 *Silla Kingdom* or 학년 *school year*, for example, the pronunciation of the initial syllable changes because of the following syllable.

5.6.4 🎧 Tensing

Basic consonants (for example, ㄷ) are sometimes pronounced—but not written—like tense consonants (for example, ㄸ).

👉 **A basic consonant becomes tense after another basic consonant**
When basic consonants like ㄱ, ㄷ, ㅂ, ㅈ or ㅅ follow another basic consonant, they become "tense." Remember that this is just the pronunciation; the spelling does not change.

학교 [학꾜]
school

듣도록 [듣또록]
so that you'll hear

학생 [학쌩]
student

찾지요? [찯찌요]
looking for (it), right?

읽고 [일꼬]
read-and

찼다 [찯따]
kicked

👉 **ㄷ, ㅅ and ㅈ become tense after ㄹ**
Weird as it sounds, tongue-tip sounds like ㄷ, ㅅ and ㅈ become ㄸ, ㅆ and ㅉ after a ㄹ.

절대	[절때]	*never*
출장	[출짱]	*business trip*
홀수	[홀쑤]	*odd number*
글자	[글짜]	*letter/character/syllable*

However, ㄱ and ㅂ are not pronounced with the tongue tip, so they are not subject to this change.

갈비	[갈비]	*rib*
달걀	[달걀]	*egg*
얼굴	[얼굴]	*face*
일본	[일본]	*Japan*

5.7   Consonant changes in compound words

The word "compound" means two words are put together to form a new word. In English, *book + case* is a compound. There are a few pronunciation rules in Korean that specifically relate to compound words.

5.7.1   🎧 Tensing of basic consonants in noun + noun compounds

The basic consonants ㄱ, ㄷ, ㅂ, ㅅ and ㅈ at the beginning of a noun are *pronounced* as tense [ㄲ, ㄸ, ㅃ, ㅆ and ㅉ] when they come after another independent word. (What counts as a "word" depends on the Korean native speaker's judgment: parts of words borrowed from Chinese, for example, are not considered independent words.) So, the exact same spelling can be read in two different ways, one with a tense consonant sound and the other with a basic consonant sound. This means most of the time when you hear a tense consonant in the second part of a compound, you can assume that it is not *written* as a tense consonant. (But it is always best to look up the spelling.)

금값	[금깝]	*cost of gold*	←	금	*gold* +	값	*price*
			vs.				
금관	[금관]	*golden crown*	←	금	*gold* +	관	*crown*

(관 is not a separate word to Koreans, whereas 값 *price* is.)

장독	[장똑]	*crock for condiments*	←	장	*condiment* +	독	*crock*
			vs.				
장도	[장도]	*long sword*	←	장	*long* +	도	*sword*

(도 is not a separate word to Koreans, whereas 독 *crock* is.)

안방	[안빵]	*master bedroom*	←	안	*inside* +	방	*room*
			vs.				
안경	[안경]	*eyeglasses*	←	안	*eye* +	경	*mirror*

(경 is not a separate word to Koreans, whereas 방 *room* is.)

잠자리	[잠짜리]	*place for sleeping*	←	잠	*sleep* +	자리	*place*
			vs.				
잠자리	[잠자리]	*dragonfly*					

(잠자리 is one word in Korean.)

5.7.2 🎧 ㅅ addition

If the first noun in the compound does not have a final consonant, for example as in 김치 *kimchi* or 고추 *pepper*, ㅅ is inserted *into the spelling* so the initial consonant of the second noun can be *pronounced* as tense:

김치	*kimchi*	+	국	*soup*	➡	김칫국	[김칟꾹 or 김치꾹]	*kimchi soup*
고추	*red pepper*	+	가루	*powder*	➡	고춧가루	[고춛까루 or 고추까루]	*red pepper powder*
바다	*sea*	+	가	*edge*	➡	바닷가	[바닫까 or 바다까]	*beach*
어제	*yesterday*	+	밤	*night*	➡	어젯밤	[어젣빰 or 어제빰]	*last night*
코	*nose*	+	수염	*beard*	➡	콧수염	[콛쑤염 or 코쑤염]	*mustache*

📌 **Hint for spelling**

> If you know how to spell the word for *sleep* 잠, and the word for *room/space* 자리, then you will have no problem with the spelling of 잠자리 (*sleeping space*) even if what you hear is [잠짜리]. It also works backwards: let's say you see 콧수염 (*mustache*) written or hear [콛쑤염]. You happen to know the meaning of 코 *nose* and the meaning of either 수염 (*beard/facial hair*) or 콧수염 (*mustache*), so you can probably guess that the ㅅ is added to make the pronunciation turn out to be [콛쑤염], with tensing in the second part.

5.7.3 Other additions

Sometimes sounds are *added* rather than changed when they are next to each other in compounds.

5.7.3.1 🎧 ㄹ addition

In a noun compound, if the first noun ends in ㄹ and the second noun begins with a vowel syllable of the 이 kind, which includes 야 (이 + 아), 여 (이 + 어), 요 (이 + 오) and 유 (이 + 우), the ㄹ is doubled (ㄹㄹ) in the pronunciation:

물	*water*	+	약	*medicine*	➡	물약	[물략]	*liquid medicine*
할	*do-to*	+	일	*work, job, matter*	➡	할일	[할릴]	*things to do, chores*
별	*special, other*	+	일	*work, job, matter*	➡	별일	[별릴]	*special matter*
구팔	*9, 8*	+	육칠	*6, 7*	➡	구팔육칠	[구팔륙칠]	*9, 8, 6, 7*

5.7.3.2 🎧 ㄴ addition

In a noun compound, if the first noun ends in a consonant other than ㄹ and the second noun begins with a 이 vowel syllable (including 야, 여, 요 and 유), a ㄴ sound is added (only in the pronunciation):

색	*color*	+	연필	*pencil*		➡	색연필	[생년필]	*colored pencil*	
중국	*China*	+	요리	*cuisine*		➡	중국 요리	[중궁뇨리]	*Chinese cuisine*	
식용	*eat-for*	+	유	*oil*		➡	식용유	[시굥뉴]	*cooking oil*	
깨	*sesame*	+	ㅅ	+ 잎 *leaf*	➡	깻잎	[깬닙]	*sesame leaf*	

5.7.3.4 🎧 이 suffix

When they come before an 이 suffix (of any kind), ㄷ is pronounced as ㅈ and ㅌ is pronounced ㅊ.

맏	*the first*	+	이 person suffix	➡	맏이	*the eldest*	pronounced [마지]
굳	*hard*	+	이 adverb suffix	➡	굳이	*obstinately*	pronounced [구지]
밭	*field*	+	이 subject particle	➡	밭이	*the field is...*	pronounced [바치]
같	*same*	+	이 adverb suffix	➡	같이	*together, alike*	pronounced [가치]

5.8 🎧 Unexpected pronunciations

Finally, here are a couple of pronunciation rules that are a bit unexpected.

☞ **Basic consonants become tense when emotionally loaded**

Sometimes, basic consonants are pronounced as tense for emphasis or emotional effect:

세다	[쎄다]	*strong*		작다	[짝따]	*small*
진하다	[찐하다]	*thick, strong*		좀	[쫌]	*a bit*
생으로	[쌩으로]	*raw*		질기다	[찔기다]	*tough, chewy*
공짜로	[꽁짜로]	*for free*		줄었어	[쭈러써]	*It shrank.*
닦아	[따까]	*Wipe it! (Clean it up!)*		버스	[뻐쓰]	*bus*
잘렸나?	[짤련나]	*Was it cut?*		내버려 둬	[냅뻐려 ᵂ도]	*Leave it.*

☞ **의 is not always [의]**

의 is pronounced as 의 only when it is the first syllable of a word in the Seoul dialect. Anywhere else in a sentence, it is usually pronounced as something between [의] and [이]. Other dialects regularly pronounce it as [이].

의사	[의사]	*doctor*		의자	[의자]	*chair*
편의	[편이]	*convenience*		강의	[강이]	*lecture*

If 의 expresses possession (the same as *'s* in English), it is pronounced as a vowel close to [에]:

선생님의 책	[선생님에 책]	*the teacher's book*
우리의 소원	[우리에 소원]	*our wish*
123-4567	[일리사메 사오륙칠]	*(telephone number)*

If ㅢ comes after a consonant, it is pronounced as [이]:

희망	[히망]	*hope*
희소식	[히소식]	*good, happy news*
흰색	[힌색]	*the color white*

5.9 🎧 All together!

As a result of the various pronunciation principles, there can be word pairs with different spellings but the same pronunciation:

[소라]	솔아	*pine tree-vocative particle*	[소라]	소라	*conch*
[보리]	볼이	*cheek-subject particle*	[보리]	보리	*barley*
[밤만]	밥만	*rice-only*	[밤만]	밤만	*chestnut-only*
[밥또]	밥도	*rice-also*	[밥또]	밥 또	*rice again*

On the other hand, do be careful with words that may sound similar at first, but make a world of difference to native speakers:

노라]	놀아	*play*	[놀라]	놀라	*surprised*
[노래]	노래	*song, yellow*	[노으래]	놓으래	*(someone says) let go*
[마나]	많아	*plentiful*	[만나]	만나	*to meet*
[팔리]	팔리	*to be sold*	[빨리]	빨리	*quickly*

Practice 1 **Cover the right-hand column and try pronouncing these words correctly. Check your pronunciation by listening to the audio recording.**

못 먹어	*cannot eat*	[몬머거, 몸머거]
잤는지	*whether you slept*	[잔는지]
윗니	*upper teeth*	[윈니]
윗물	*water from the upstream*	[윈물, 윔물]
몇 해	*how many years, few years*	[며태]
못 해	*cannot do*	[모태]
웃옷	*top, shirt, upper garment*	[우돋]
웃었어	*laughed*	[우서써]
못 읽어	*cannot read*	[모딜거 or 몬닐거]
옷 입어	*wear clothes*	[오디버]
갇히다	*be locked up*	[가치다]
같이	*together*	[가치]
달아	*sweet, hang (it)*	[다라]
달라	*different*	[달라]

The pronunciation rules introduced in this chapter may seem like a lot to learn all at once, and it is! You can use this section as a warm-up for now. Then later you can come back to it as a reference when you are learning new vocabulary along with its pronunciation and spelling, and remind yourself why they sometimes don't quite match up perfectly—"Oh, yeah! The Spillover Rule!"

6 READING AND WRITING PRACTICE

Now that you know all the Hangul letters, writing rules and pronunciation principles, let's practice some useful daily words and phrases. For each exercise in this section, listen to the online audio and practice reading, writing and pronouncing the words.

6.1 🎧 Greetings and useful daily expressions

1. 안녕하세요. Hello.

| 안 | 녕 | 하 | 세 | 요 | | | | | | | | | | | | | | | |

2. 안녕히 가세요. Goodbye (to someone who is leaving).

| 안 | 녕 | 히 | 가 | 세 | 요 | | | | | | | | | | | | | | |

3. 안녕히 계세요. Goodbye (to someone who is staying).

| 안 | 녕 | 히 | 계 | 세 | 요 | | | | | | | | | | | | | | |

4. 감사합니다. Thank you.

| 감 | 사 | 합 | 니 | 다 | | | | | | | | | | | | | | | |

5. 아니에요. No problem.

| 아 | 니 | 에 | 요 | | | | | | | | | | | | | | | | |

6. 죄송합니다. I'm sorry.

| 죄 | 송 | 합 | 니 | 다 | | | | | | | | | | | | | | | |

7. 괜찮아요. That's ok.

| 괜 | 찮 | 아 | 요 | | | | | | | | | | | | | | | | |

8. 실례합니다. Excuse me.

| 실 | 례 | 합 | 니 | 다 | | | | | | | | | | | | | | | |

9. 네. Yes.

| 네 | | | | | | | | | | | | | | | | | | | |

10. 아니요. No.

| 아 | 니 | 요 | | | | | | | | | | | | | | | | | |

6.2 🎧 Family members and pets

1. 할머니 grandmother

할	머	니												

2. 할아버지 grandfather

할	아	버	지											

3. 어머니 mother

어	머	니												

4. 엄마 mom

엄	마													

5. 아버지 father

아	버	지												

6. 아빠 dad

아	빠													

7. 오빠 older brother of female

오	빠													

8. 언니 older sister of female

언	니													

9. 형 older brother of male

형														

10. 누나 older sister of male

누	나													

11. 여동생 younger sister

여	동	생												

12. 남동생 younger brother

남	동	생												

13. 남편   husband

남	편													

14. 아내   wife

아	내													

15. 딸   daughter

딸														

16. 아들   son

아	들													

17. 고양이   cat

고	양	이									

18. 개   dog

개														

FAMILY TREE

6.3 🎧 Days of the week

1. 일요일 Sunday

일	요	일																		

2. 월요일 Monday

월	요	일																		

3. 화요일 Tuesday

화	요	일																		

4. 수요일 Wednesday

수	요	일																		

5. 목요일 Thursday

목	요	일																		

6. 금요일 Friday

금	요	일																		

7. 토요일 Saturday

토	요	일																		

6.4 Numbers

The Korean language uses two different sets of words for numbers: a Korean set that is native to the language, and a Sino-Korean set, which was borrowed from the Chinese language long ago. Let's learn both sets.

6.4.1 Sino-Korean numbers

The Sino-Korean numbers are used for page numbers, the floors in a building and the minutes in telling time. They are also used to name months and to read dates and years; for telephone numbers, room numbers, license plate numbers, ID numbers and numbers above 100.

🎧 **Listen to the audio and practice reading, writing and pronouncing the following numbers.**

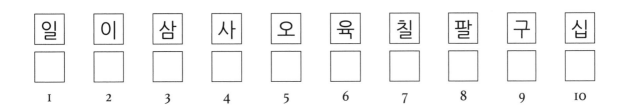

일	이	삼	사	오	육	칠	팔	구	십
☐	☐	☐	☐	☐	☐	☐	☐	☐	☐
1	2	3	4	5	6	7	8	9	10

✍ **Write these license plate numbers in Korean.**

1. 34 가 2195

| | 가 | | | | |

2. 22 루 1328

| | 루 | | | |

3. 89 버 2341

| | 버 | | | | |

4. 54 허 3978

| | 허 | | | |

5. 69 서 2384

| | 서 | | | | |

6. 84 주 65213

| | 주 | | | | | |

6.4.2 Native Korean numbers

There is also a set of numbers that are native to the Korean language. Native numbers are used to count items.

🎧 **Listen to the audio and practice reading, writing and pronouncing the following numbers.**

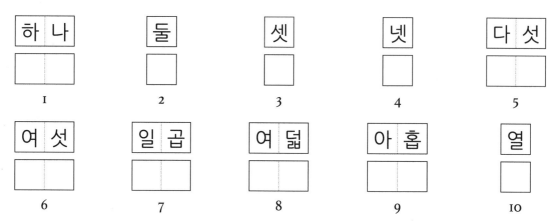

✍ **Count the following candies (count in Korean) and fill in the blanks with the appropriate native numbers.**

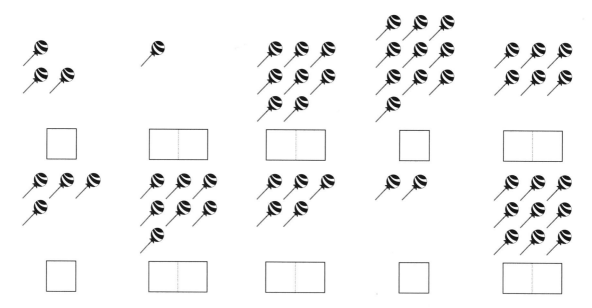

6.5 🎧 Korean cities

I. 서울   Seoul

서울									

2. 광주   Gwangju

광주									

3. 부산   Busan

부산									

4. 강릉   Gangneung

강릉									

5. 인천   Incheon

인천									

6. 제주   Jeju

제주									

7. 대전   Daejeon

대전									

8 개성   Gaeseong

개성									

9. 대구   Daegu

대구									

IO. 평양   Pyongyang

평양									

6.6 🎧 Places in town

1. 백화점 department store

백화점

2. 식당 restaurant

식당

3. 영화관 movie theater

영화관

4. 피씨방 PC room (game café)

피씨방

5. 노래방 karaoke room

노래방

6. 미장원 hair salon

미장원

7. 호텔 hotel

호텔

8. 기차역 train station

기차역

9. 지하철역 subway station

지하철역

10. 버스정류장 bus stop

버스정류장

11. 학교 school

학교

12. 약국　pharmacy

약	국										

13. 병원　hospital

병	원										

14. 은행　bank

은	행										

15. 경찰서　police station

경	찰	서						

16. 편의점　convenience store

편	의	점						

17. 세탁소　dry cleaner's

세	탁	소						

18. 박물관　museum

박	물	관						

19. 공항　airport

공	항										

20. 대학교　college, university

대	학	교						

21. 서점　bookstore

서	점										

22. 소방서　fire station

소	방	서						

23. 우체국　post office

우	체	국						

6.7 🎧 Transportation

1. 차 car

차

2. 버스 bus

버스

3. 기차 train

기차

4. 지하철 subway

지하철

5. 비행기 airplane

비행기

6. 고속버스 express bus

고속버스

7. 택시 taxi

택시

8. 공항버스 airport bus

공항버스

9. 자전거 bicycle

자전거

10. 배 boat, ship

배

11. 한강유람선 Han River cruise

한강유람선

6.8 Parts of the body

🎧 **Listen to the audio and label the diagram with the Korean word for each part of the body.**

eye	눈	nose	코	mouth	입	ear	귀
face	얼굴	head	머리	neck	목	shoulder	어깨
arm	팔	hand	손	stomach	배	back	등
waist	허리	leg	다리	foot	발	knee	무릎

6.9 🎧 Clothes

1. 티셔츠 T-shirt

티	셔	츠						

2. 치마 skirt

치	마							

3. 반팔셔츠 short-sleeved shirt

반	팔	셔	츠				

4. 바지 pants

바	지							

5. 재킷 jacket

재	킷							

6. 청바지 jeans

청	바	지						

7. 코트 coat

코	트							

8. 모자 hat, cap

모	자							

9. 원피스 dress

원	피	스						

10. 신발 shoes

신	발							

11. 운동화 sneakers

운	동	화					

12. 블라우스   blouse

블	라	우	스												

13. 카디건   cardigan

카	디	건												

14. 수영복   swimsuit

수	영	복												

15. 레깅스   leggings

레	깅	스												

16. 반바지   short pants

반	바	지												

17. 청재킷   jean jacket

청	재	킷												

6.10 🎧 At a Korean restaurant

1. 불고기　bulgogi

불	고	기										

2. 갈비　galbi

갈	비												

3. 냉면　cold noodle soup

냉	면												

4. 김밥　kimbap

김	밥												

5. 된장찌개　soybean stew

된	장	찌	개								

6. 김치찌개　kimchi stew

김	치	찌	개								

7. 육개장　spicy beef soup (yukgaejang)

육	개	장										

8. 비빔밥　bibimbap

비	빔	밥											

9. 떡볶이　stir-fried rice cake (ddukbokki)

떡	볶	이										

10. 해물파전　seafood scallion pancake

해	물	파	전								

11. 삼계탕　chicken ginseng soup

삼	계	탕										

7 Typing in Korean

There are two different keyboard layouts used in Korea, 2-set and 3-set; the 2-set is more widely used. You can install the 2-set layout on your PC or Mac or on your mobile device. Note that Korean people do not type Korean using a romanization keyboard as it is relatively easy to type in Korean: the consonant keys are on the left of the keyboard and the vowel keys on the right. When you type each character in order, the computer arranges them into syllable blocks. Remember to type the ㅇ of vowel syllables. Do you remember that ㅗ always pairs with ㅏ, ㅑ, ㅐ and ㅒ while ㅜ pairs with ㅓ, ㅕ, ㅔ and ㅖ? Computers *will not* combine ㅗ with the ㅓ-based vowels, nor will it combine ㅜ with the ㅏ-based vowels into a single syllable.

The shift key is used to type tense consonants and the two vowels ㅐ and ㅔ. For other complex vowel syllables, type the two-vowel combinations. For example, to type 와, type ㅇ, ㅗ and ㅏ.

If you feel that it is hard to memorize the new keyboard layout, you can purchase Korean keyboard stickers and put them on your keyboard.

~ `	! 1	@ 2	# 3	$ 4	% 5	^ 6	& 7	* 8	(9	) 0	_ -	+ =		\	←
Tab ↔	ㅃ ㅂ	ㅉ ㅈ	ㄸ ㄷ	ㄲ ㄱ	ㅆ ㅅ	ㅛ ㅛ	ㅕ ㅕ	ㅑ ㅑ	ㅒ ㅐ	ㅖ ㅔ	{ [	}]		Enter
Caps Lock	ㅁ	ㄴ	ㅇ	ㄹ	ㅎ	ㅗ	ㅓ	ㅏ	ㅣ	: ;	" '			↵
↑	ㅋ	ㅌ	ㅊ	ㅍ	ㅠ	ㅜ	ㅡ	< ,	> .	? /	↑			

ANSWER KEY

Page 22, Practice 2

1. 아
2. 으
3. 오
4. 어
5. 아이
6. 우아
7. 어
8. 에이

Page 22, Practice 3

1. 에
2. 어
3. 우

Page 30, Practice 2

1. 여
2. 요
3. 어
4. 유
5. 에
6. 얘기

Page 30, Practice 3

1. 유
2. 여
3. 요
4. 예
5. 얘
6. 야

Page 38, Practice 2

1. 아
2. 워
3. 의
4. 워
5. 웨
6. 외

Page 39, Practice 4

1. 의
2. 외
3. 왜
4. 워
5. 왜
6. 위

Page 54, Practice 5

1. 사
2. 바
3. 자
4. 마
5. 다
6. 하
7. 나
8. 바

Page 59, Practice 1

ㄱ	ㄷ	ㅂ	ㅈ
ㅋ	ㅌ	ㅍ	ㅊ

Page 59, practice 2

Page 59, Practice 3

1. 파
2. 카
3. 타
4. 차

Page 62, Practice 3

1. 다
2. 나
3. 마
4. 하
5. 카
6. 다
7. 자
8. 파

Page 62, Practice 4

1. 자
2. 마
3. 파
4. 바
5. 사
6. 타

Page 69, Practice 3

1. 따
2. 싸
3. 가
4. 따
5. 아빠
6. 차다

Page 69, Practice 4

1. 싸
2. 짜
3. 까
4. 따
5. 빠
6. 짜

Page 69, Practice 1

Basic/Plain	Aspirated (burst of air)	Tense
가	카	까
바	파	빠
다	타	따
사		싸
자	차	짜

Page 80, Practice 2

1. a
2. b
3. a
4. a
5. b
6. b
7. b
8. a

Page 80, Practice 3

1. 마
2. 지
3. 모
4. 두
5. 셔
6. 토
7. 즈
8. 피
9. 스
10. 케

Page 81, Practice 5

1. 시카고
2. 제주
3. 파리
4. 도쿄
5. 하노이
6. 제네바
7. 자카르타
8. 마드리드
9. 시드니

Page 85, Practice 1

1. b
2. b
3. a
4. a
5. b
6. b
7. a
8. a

Page 85, Practice 2

1. 과
2. 배
3. 위
4. 돼
5. 쥐
6. 개
7. 화
8. 의
9. 배

Page 95, Practice 1

1. 감
2. 살
3. 잠
4. 박
5. 빛
6. 넣
7. 짐
8. 숲

Page 95, Practice 2

1. c. 임
2. a. 업
3. b. 솝
4. a. 각

"Books to Span the East and West"

Tuttle Publishing was founded in 1832 in the small New England town of Rutland, Vermont [USA]. Our core values remain as strong today as they were then—to publish best-in-class books which bring people together one page at a time. In 1948, we established a publishing office in Japan—and Tuttle is now a leader in publishing English-language books about the arts, languages and cultures of Asia. The world has become a much smaller place today and Asia's economic and cultural influence has grown. Yet the need for meaningful dialogue and information about this diverse region has never been greater. Over the past seven decades, Tuttle has published thousands of books on subjects ranging from martial arts and paper crafts to language learning and literature—and our talented authors, illustrators, designers and photographers have won many prestigious awards. We welcome you to explore the wealth of information available on Asia at www.tuttlepublishing.com.

Published by Tuttle Publishing, an imprint of Periplus Editions (HK) Ltd.

www.tuttlepublishing.com

Copyright © 2022 Emily Curtis, Haewon Cho and Soohee Kim.
All rights reserved.

Library of Congress Catalog-in-Publication Data in progress

ISBN 978-0-8048-5290-6

Illustration credits: Photos p. 2–5 top; bottom illustrations p. 11–28; illustrations p. 30–40; bottom illustrations p. 43–52; illustrations p. 54; bottom illustrations p. 55–58; illustrations p. 59–62; bottom illustrations p. 63–67; illustrations p. 69–114; p. 121–23: all Shutterstock. Page 5 bottom, page 125, Wikimedia Commons.

Distributed by
North America, Latin America & Europe
Tuttle Publishing
364 Innovation Drive
North Clarendon,
VT 05759-9436 U.S.A.
Tel: 1 (802) 773-8930; Fax: 1 (802) 773-6993
info@tuttlepublishing.com
www.tuttlepublishing.com

Asia Pacific
Berkeley Books Pte. Ltd.
3 Kallang Sector #04-01
Singapore 349278
Tel: (65) 6741-2178; Fax: (65) 6741-2179
inquiries@periplus.com.sg
www.tuttlepublishing.com

25 24 23 23 22   5 4 3 2 1
Printed in Singapore   2202TP

TUTTLE PUBLISHING® is a registered trademark of Tuttle Publishing, a division of Periplus Editions (HK) Ltd.